ADMINISTERING SUCCESSFUL PROGRAMS FOR ADULTS

Promoting Excellence in Adult, Community, and Continuing Education

The Professional Practices in Adult Education and Human Resource Development Series explores issues and concerns of practitioners who work in the broad range of settings in adult and continuing education and human resource development.

The books are intended to provide information and strategies on how to make practice more effective for professionals and those they serve. They are written from a practical viewpoint and provide a forum for instructors, administrators, policy makers, counselors, trainers, managers, program and organizational developers, instructional designers, and other related professionals.

Editorial correspondence should be sent to the Editor-in-Chief:

Michael W. Galbraith
Florida Atlantic University
Department of Educational Leadership
College of Education
Boca Raton, FL 33431

ADMINISTERING SUCCESSFUL PROGRAMS FOR ADULTS

Promoting Excellence in Adult, Community, and Continuing Education

Michael W. Galbraith
Burton R. Sisco
Lucy Madsen Guglielmino

KRIEGER PUBLISHING COMPANY
MALABAR, FLORIDA
1997

Original Edition   1997

Printed and Published by
KRIEGER PUBLISHING COMPANY
KRIEGER DRIVE
MALABAR, FLORIDA 32950

FROM A DECLARATION OF PRINCIPLES JOINTLY ADOPTED BY A COM-
MITTEE OF THE AMERICAN BAR ASSOCIATION AND A COMMITTEE OF
PUBLISHERS:
This publication is designed to provide accurate and authoritative information in regard to the subject matter covered. It is sold with the understanding that the publisher
is not engaged in rendering legal, accounting, or other professional service. If legal
advice or other expert assistance is required, the services of a competent professional
person should be sought.

Galbraith, Michael W.
    Administering successful programs for adults : promoting excellence
in adult, community, and continuing education / Michael W. Galbraith,
Burton R. Sisco, Lucy Madsen Guglielmino. — Original ed.
    p.   cm. — (The professional practices in adult education and
human resource development series)
    Includes bibliographical references and index.
    ISBN 0-89464-886-1
    1. Adult education—Administration.   2. Continuing education—
Administration.   I. Sisco, Burton, 1951-   .   II. Guglielmino,
Lucy Madsen.   III. Title.   IV. Series.
LC5225.A34G35   1997
374′.0068—dc20   96-28076
                                                                CIP

10 9 8 7 6 5 4 3 2

CONTENTS

PREFACE

Often professionals within adult, community, and continuing education are thrust into administrative roles and positions as a result of intentional or unintentional agency and organizational circumstances. Others seek an administrative position as an advancement in their career path.

Administrators in adult, community, and continuing education settings, for the most part, are guided by general knowledge, concepts, theories, literature, and practices gleaned from related fields. Although the literature to inform and guide the administrator has increased over the last three decades, there has not been an abundance of writings that provide the specialized knowledge that deals directly with administration in adult, community, and continuing education. With the realization that a vast majority of practitioners in adult, community, and continuing education function as the director, manager, or coordinator of agencies or programs sometime during their professional lives, it is surprising that so little attention has been given to assist and guide individuals in this area of inquiry to enhance their proficiencies. Knox (1991) states that it is "paradoxical that practitioners seek more attention for the administrative role that scholars are providing" (p. 217). Few books have been written that address the process of administration and its related major functions specifically for the fields of adult, community, and continuing education. This book adds to the specialized knowledge base essential for administrators who promote and strive for excellence within their agencies, organizations, and programs.

Administering Successful Programs for Adults provides a practical orientation as well as a conceptual framework for understanding the administrative process. It examines the primary elements, functions, and processes involved with effective administration of adult, community, and continuing education agencies and organizations. This book assists individuals who are already administrators to better understand and perhaps enhance their own skills and proficiencies through a reflective process. In addition, it benefits those professionals who have recently become administrators to gain new insights into the administrative process and the essential skills, functions, and proficiencies necessary to maintain effectiveness.

The authors recognize that the topics in this book could easily be expanded into several volumes. It is our purpose to examine in broad strokes the tasks, functions, and skills associated with the administrative process and to provide within the text the most salient references that will allow the reader to examine selected topics in-depth.

Chapter 1 focuses on the administrator and examines the settings and contexts in which the administrative role is carried out. In addition, it details the characteristics as well as the most prominent functions, tasks, and skills for the administrator within adult, community, and continuing education agencies and organizations. Chapter 1 also provides a self-assessment inventory that allows the reader to discover the function and skill areas that are highly developed and those that need some additional attention in relationship to the importance of a particular administrative role. Using the inventory results, the reader can use the book in a proactive manner and read those chapters that are of greatest interest or need.

Approaches to administration are explored in Chapter 2. The classical, human relations, organization behavior, contingency, and systems perspectives are examined in relation to their appropriateness for adult, community, and continuing education. The chapter emphasizes an integrative approach which will allow adaptation to change.

Chapter 3 addresses the administrator's role and involvement in the process of determining program content. A multistage process (macro level and micro level) is presented as a way of determining program content. Emphasis is placed on the macro level since it is there that the program administrator's involvement is the greatest.

Understanding budgetary and financial matters is the focus of Chapter 4. A description of the purposes and types of budgets is presented along with some definitions of key terms associated with budgeting and financing. Some useful tips on how to develop a successful budget are presented as well as how to augment funding through the identification of income sources such as grants or external awards.

Selecting and developing staff is an essential function of administrators in adult, community, and continuing education agencies and organizations. The purpose of Chapter 5 is to present a staffing plan that articulates a process of identifying the roles and responsibilities of staff, an approach for selecting staff, strategies for communicating job expectations, and suggestions for developing staff.

The success and effectiveness of large, medium, or small organizations depend greatly upon how well they engage in marketing and public relations efforts. Chapter 6 is dedicated to the understanding of marketing and the essential elements of a marketing plan and promotional strategies. The process of public relations is also explored and effective strategies are offered.

Chapter 7 is devoted to the process of evaluating programs for adults. Information on various types of evaluation are presented along with some questions that will assist in the design and application of an evaluation plan. Productive use of evaluation findings by the administrator concludes the chapter.

Legal issues and ethical considerations is the focus of Chapter 8. Within the chapter affirmative action and equal employment opportunity guidelines related to hiring practices for personnel are discussed as well as an overview of the Americans with Disabilities Act of 1990 and some implications associated with the law. Finally, certain ethical dilemmas confronting the administrator are examined.

Chapter 9 is concerned with maintaining effectiveness as an administrator through professional development of yourself and others. The characteristics of a learning organization and the use of its precepts to improve the organization is discussed. Attention shifts to preparing performance development plans as tools for growing, changing, and dealing with the task of remaining current in the information age. The chapter concludes with a brief annotated listing of resources found to be particularly helpful in ensuring administrative and organizational success.

The audience for this book extends from graduate students to seasoned professionals who desire more practitioner-oriented information about the administrative process within adult, community, and continuing education settings. Newly appointed administrators should find the information valuable in their efforts to understand and implement sound administrative processes that promote effective programs for adults. Experienced administrators may discover new insights that affect the way they conduct their practices.

Faculty in adult, community, and continuing education graduate programs will find this book to be a useful primary text for courses concerned with the topic of organization and administration of programs for adults. Seminar and workshop leaders for professional schools and training programs should find helpful information about the administrative process they can utilize in conducting training and development sessions. In addition, individuals who have a general interest in administration will discover the merit of this book as a general resource.

The authors recognize the complexity of the dynamics involved within administration. We have attempted to draw out and examine some of the primary elements that constitute this process. It is our hope that such an effort will assist those professionals who study the administrative process or are engaged in an active agenda of administering programs to better understand and promote sound administrative practices that will strengthen adult, community, and continuing education programs for adults.

ACKNOWLEDGMENTS

The authors wish to thank some very special colleagues for their input and assistance in the development of this book. Our sincere gratitude goes to Dr. Valerie C. Bryan for sharing her time, information, and materials. To Susan F. Schulz for reading and making valuable suggestions on several of the chapters, and to Debra L. Hargrove and Marcia Brooker for their computer expertise on some of the graphs and figures, we offer a special thank you. To our graduate students who have read the manuscript, we say thank you for your valuable suggestions and the kind challenges put forth. As always, a sincere thank you to Mary Roberts and Marie Bowles of Krieger Publishing Company for their invaluable assistance and insights. A special thank you goes to Kim Krause for her detailed and attentive critique of the manuscript.

From Michael W. Galbraith:

A special thanks to T.J. Galbraith for loving me through the ebb and flow of life's journey and to my son John Michael for helping me keep a balance and focus on the importance of playing in the park.

From Burton R. Sisco:

To my wife Ellen Sisco, my son Geoff, and my daughter Jessica whose care, patience, and understanding made this project possible, this book is lovingly dedicated.

From Lucy Madsen Guglielmino:

Many thanks are due to Paul Guglielmino, my son Joe, and my daughter Meg who put up with my strange sleeping and writing patterns and provided unfailing support during the preparation of this book. A loving thank you to my mother and father, Margaret and Robert Madsen, who awakened and nurtured an early love of words which has persisted throughout my life, enriching it greatly.

THE AUTHORS

Michael W. Galbraith is Professor of Adult Education in the Department of Educational Leadership at Florida Atlantic University in Boca Raton, Florida. He received his B.Ed. degree (1973) in social studies education and an M.Ed. degree (1981) in Gerontology\Social Foundations from the University of Toledo, and his Ed.D. (1984) in adult education from Oklahoma State University.

Galbraith's primary teaching and writing activities have been in the areas of facilitating adult learning, critical issues, mentoring, and community adult education. He has published numerous articles, books, book chapters, and monographs including *Mentoring: New Strategies and Challenges* (1995, with Norman H. Cohen), *Confronting Controversies in Challenging Times* (1992, with Burton R. Sisco), *Education in the Rural American Community* (1992), *Facilitating Adult Learning* (1991), *Education Through Community Organizations* (1990), *Adult Learning Methods* (1990), *Elder Abuse: Perspectives on an Emerging Crisis* (1986), and *Professional Certification: Implications for Adult Education and HRD* (1986, with Jerry W. Gilley).

Galbraith has received numerous state, regional, and national awards for his leadership and service to the field of adult education. He was the recipient of the American Association for Adult and Continuing Education Membership Award seven times and was presented with the "Outstanding Adult Educator Award" from the Missouri and Pennsylvania professional associations. He serves as editor-in-chief for the national book series "Professional Practices in Adult Education and Human Resource Development" as well as on the journal editorial boards for *Adult Education Quarterly*, *Adult Learning*, and *PAACE Journal of Lifelong Learning*.

Galbraith has served on the faculties of Temple University, University of Missouri-Columbia, and Oklahoma State University. Before journeying into higher education, he served in various administrative roles in several community-based organizations.

Burton R. Sisco is Professor of Adult Education and Associate Dean for Graduate Studies and Research for the College of Education at the University of Wyoming. He received his B. A. degree (1973) in history and an M.Ed. degree (1977) in teacher education at the University of Vermont, and his Ed.D. degree (1981) in adult education from Syracuse University.

Sisco's primary teaching activities have been in the area of adult learning and lifespan development, historical foundations of adult education, program planning and evaluation, and teaching adults. His research interests lie in the areas of adult cognition, self-directed learning, and teaching effectiveness. Among his books are *Individualizing Instruction: Making Learning Personal, Empowering, and Successful* (1990, with Roger Hiemstra), and *Confronting Controversies in Challenging Times* (1992, with Michael W. Galbraith).

Sisco has held numerous leadership positions with the American Association for Adult and Continuing Education. He is past editor of the Mountain Plains Adult Education Association *Journal of Adult Education*, and has served as book review editor for the *Adult Literacy and Basic Education* journal, and on the editorial board of the *Adult Education Quarterly*.

Before coming to the University of Wyoming, Sisco served on the faculty at Syracuse University from 1983–1985. In addition, he was a program development specialist in the Division of Continuing Education at the University of Vermont from 1979–1983.

Lucy Madsen Guglielmino is Professor of Adult and Community Education in the Department of Educational Leadership at Florida Atlantic University in Boca Raton, Florida. She received her B.A. degree (1966) in English and Education from Furman University and an M.Ed. degree (1973) in English and Education from the Savannah Graduate Center, and her Ed.D. (1977) in adult education from the University of Georgia.

Guglielmino's teaching areas are focused toward program and curriculum planning, organization and administration of adult education, and adult learning. Her primary research area has been centered on self-direction in learning. She is the author of *The Self-Directed Learning Readiness Scale*, which was developed in 1977 and has been translated into nine languages and used in more than two dozen countries. Guglielmino is the author of *Adult ESL Instruction: A Sourcebook* (1991) and numerous monographs, articles, and book chapters as well as several videotapes.

Guglielmino has received several awards for her teaching, research, and service, including being selected for the Florida Adult and Community Education Hall of Fame, *Outstanding Young Women of America, Who's Who in American Education, 2000 Notable American Women,* and the *International Directory of Distinguished Leadership*. At Florida Atlantic University she has administered grant-funded programs, served as Acting Associate Dean of the College of Education, and was the first woman chair of the Department of Educational Leadership. In addition to her professorial responsibilities, she currently directs the Ernest O. Melby Community Education Center.

CHAPTER 1

The Administrator

To a large extent, success of adult, community, and continuing education organizations depends upon the skill, knowledge, and political savvy of individuals who hold the administrative roles. Becoming an effective and efficient administrator depends upon an individual's ability to gain general knowledge of administration, to recognize what distinguishes adult, community, and continuing education administrators from other types of administrators, and to directly relate this knowledge and information to a specialized agency, organization, or program.

The amount of literature detailing the administrative process in adult, community, and continuing education has increased in recent years, although not very rapidly (i.e., Courtenay, 1990, 1993; Edelson, 1992; Johnson, 1990; Knox, 1991, 1993; Kowalski, 1988; Mulcrone, 1993; Porter, 1982; Sergiovanni, 1993; Smith & Offerman, 1989). Given the enhanced awareness and prevalence of adult, community, and continuing education administrative careers and the concern with what to do and techniques for how to be administrators, one would expect to find greater attention paid to these matters in the literature.

Interestingly, most graduates of university programs in adult, community, and continuing education work in administrative roles. However, they have had to study noncontext-specific administrative literature with the hope of finding meaning and the relationship to their specific administrative roles.

This chapter will examine the settings or contexts in which you may find yourself carrying out an administrative role. In addition, it will detail the characteristics as well as the most salient functions, tasks, and skills essential for administrators who work within adult, community, and continuing education settings. A self-assessment inventory is also presented that will allow you to discover the function and skill areas that are highly developed, those that need more attention, and realistically determine what functions and skills are most important for your particular administrative role (see Appendix A at the end of this chapter). From the inventory findings, each individual can utilize the book in a proactive manner and read those chapters that are of greatest interest or need.

THE CONTEXTS OF THE ADMINISTRATOR

An array of possible adult, community, and continuing educational settings exist in which you could find yourself performing administrative tasks and functions. A number of typologies have been put forth in an attempt to explain the providers of adult, community, and continuing education (Apps, 1989; Darkenwald & Merriam, 1982; Kowalski, 1988; Schroeder, 1970). Each framework categorizes organizations by whether their purpose is to serve adults exclusively or if providing adult learning activities is an allied function of the organization.

For example, you may be a program coordinator within a proprietary school that provides computer training only for adults or perhaps a community education program director that provides computer training to adults but the program is located within a public high school. Several differences exist; one is a private for-profit organization and the second is a public nonprofit program that is located within an organization whose primary purpose is to serve youths but offers and serves adult learners as a secondary function. In addition, you may work as an administrator of an adult learning program in an agency or organization that is quasi-educational such as community service, cultural, health, voluntary, church, or professional agencies and organizations or for government, armed forces, unions, or correctional organizations. The above is just a brief example of contexts in which you could find yourself functioning within an administrative capacity.

To expand your awareness of the settings in which adult, community, and continuing education administration takes place we have provided an illustration of the array of possible agencies and organizations (see Figure 1.1). In the middle of Figure 1.1 we have placed the administrator with lines leading to the various agencies and organizations. No attempt is made to present the information in any particular framework. The notion is to assist you in discovering the administrative possibilities and opportunities that await within adult, community, and continuing education.

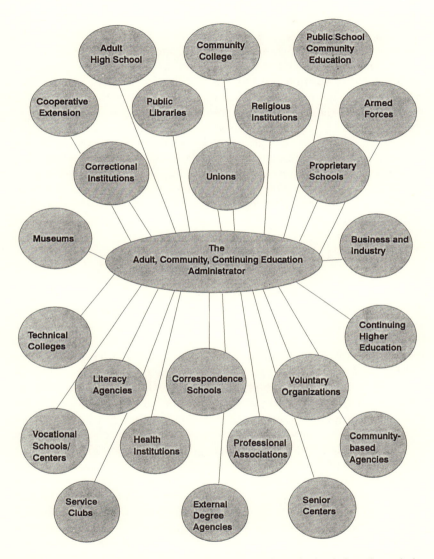

Figure 1.1 Contexts of the adult, community, and continuing education administrator

THE PROFICIENT ADMINISTRATOR

Adult, community, and continuing education administrators must devise their own approach to management, administration, and program development. Agency and organization size, location, and relationship to the parent organization will impact the approach taken. Knox (1991) suggests that "many of the distinctive characteristics that confront administrators of these agencies relate to their type of parent organization" (p. 222). Thus a broad perspective is essential in understanding what constitutes an effective administrator. This section will detail the diverse roles, characteristics, functions, and skills of the adult, community, and continuing education administrator. It is important to examine this information through the filters of what type of administrative position you hold as well as through the type of agency or organization you work for and the relationship of your program to the parent organization.

Roles and Characteristics

The role of the administrator is more than carrying out specified duties and responsibilities of a job description, it is one that is multidimensional. Adult, community, and continuing education administrators must be activists, oriented toward action and results. Effective administrators are leaders "who achieve results with and through people" (Knox, 1991, p. 222). In addition, administrators may discover other roles they play such as a figurehead who is looked to for authoritative guidance and representation of the program staff, clientele, and the public, a monitor who provides a continuous watch over the program and staff activities, a disseminator of important information to staff, parent organization, and general public, or a spokesperson who responds to and delivers official comments and information. In addition, the administrator's roles may encompass that of a strategist who guides the present and future happenings of the agency, a disturbance handler who engages in the resolution of program, clientele, staff, and the publics' concerns, a resource allocator who must determine how financial as well as human resources can best be utilized, or that of negotiator for such things as interagency cooperation ventures, resources allocation from the parent organization or board of directors, budgetary matters, promotions, salary increases, and so forth. In addition, the administrator may take on the role of supervisor in which support and guidance are provided to staff concerning their responsibilities and duties. Finally, the role of liaison provides a common connection of the whole organization to its individual parts through the establishment of communication lines and maintenance procedures that lead to mutual understanding of all involved (Mintzberg, 1973). The multifaceted roles identified would suggest that the adult, community, and continuing education administrator must be a "jack-of-all trades".

How effective each of the identified roles are realized depends upon, to some degree, what characteristics and personal qualities the administrator possesses. Eble (1992) and Knowles (1980) provide interesting lists of essential and favorable characteristics and qualities for effective administrators. Eble's list includes such qualities as:

- resourcefulness and adaptability
- courage and commitment
- interpersonal relations
- sense of direction
- organizational ability
- vigor and capacity for work
- imagination and initiative
- perseverance
- common sense
- motivation and enthusiasm
- sensitivity for colleagues
- patience
- maturity
- sense of cultural diversity
- integrity and honesty
- professionalism
- assertiveness
- poise and self-confidence
- communication skills
- judgment
- loyalty
- breadth of curiosity
- candor and openness
- sense of values
- dependability
- sense of perspective
- decisiveness
- sense of compassion

Knowles (1980) hypothesizes from his experience of over 50 years that administrators should possess the following characteristics:

- have a genuine respect for the intrinsic capacity of adults to be self-directing
- derive their greatest satisfaction as administrators and educators from accomplishment through others
- value the experience of others as a resource for accomplishing both work and learning by themselves and with others
- willing to take risks that are involved in experimenting with new ideas and new approaches, and view failures as things to be learned from rather than defensive about
- have a deep commitment to and skill in the involvement of people in organizational and educational processes

- have a deep faith in the potency of educational processes for contrib-
  uting to the solution of organizational and societal problems
- able to establish warm, empathic relationships with people of all sorts;
  to see the world through their eyes; to be a good listener
- engage in a process of continuing education for themselves

Sisco (1988) suggests another characteristic and personal quality
that is essential for adult, community, and continuing education administrators—being ethical. It is perhaps this one quality that provides the
foundation for many of the ones listed. It is a fundamental virtue that all
administrators should subscribe to since it will impact the total personal
and programmatic elements of the administrative process.

The above lists are rather extensive, however, they do present an
opportunity to examine your own characteristics and personal qualities
suggested for a proficient administrator. These identified characteristics
and qualities play a key role in the conduct of administrators and helps
determine how successful they will be in carrying out the functions of
the administrative role.

Functions

Administrative functions are those necessary elements and under-
pinnings that the administrator engages in to make the agency and program offerings successful. Courtenay (1990) evaluated nine administrative functions, through a critical analysis of the literature, thought
necessary in all organizations. He found that the nine most comprehensive functions are: developing and communicating a philosophy and mission, setting goals and objectives, planning, organizing and structuring,
leadership, staffing, budgeting, marketing, and evaluation. Courtenay
states that these functions "must be in place and operative whether the
organization delivers adult basic education or continuing higher education" (p. 63). While subsequent chapters provide more in-depth detail of
each function, a brief description of each function will now be presented.

Developing and Communicating a Philosophy and Mission

Each adult, community, and continuing education organization
should have a stated philosophy which provides for an understanding of
values, concepts, and fundamental beliefs. It is essential to discover how
the organizational philosophy relates to your philosophy as an adminis-

trator. Is it compatible or in conflict? Being compatible assists in the grounding of and support for what is asked of you. If personal and the organizational philosophy is in conflict, it provides for a dysfunction between beliefs and action thus causing incompatibility among and between the organization or program.

The mission is the organization's or program's purpose, its specific task or function with which it is charged. For example, the mission of a community education program may be to provide low-cost parenting education to economically disadvantaged adults within a specified geographical area. The function of the administrator is to assist in the development of a philosophy and a mission and to communicate them through written and verbal means to the public, as well as to all individuals associated with the organization.

Setting Goals and Objectives

Another function of the administrator is to establish goals for the organization and objectives for reaching the identified goals. A goal is a broad statement that stems from the overall mission of the organization, while objectives are statements that flow from the goal statements. For example, from our mission statement above, a goal may be to provide literacy programs as part of parenting education with several objectives being to establish five education centers around the geographical area, to enroll 20 parents in each, to train literacy volunteers, to increase the GED success rate to 100%, and so forth.

It is imperative for the administrator to be realistic about what the organization and program can engage in and be responsible for as the goals and objectives, based on standards and priorities, are established. Are the goals and objectives within the mission? Are resources available or can they be secured? Will interagency cooperation be needed to realize success? Do we know what the social context and educational needs are? What barriers will we need to overcome? Effective administrators understand the mission of their organization before investing time, energy, and resources into establishing unrealistic goals and objectives. With a clear vision, appropriate goals and objectives will be developed and realized.

Planning

After the establishment of realistic goals and objectives the process of planning how the goals and objectives will be reached goes into effect. The administrator has a major role in the planning function. Administrative involvement includes such considerations as the method of assessing community and learner needs, identifying the appropriate audience, the competition, the content that will be included, the cost, methods for delivering the program, staffing as related to cost, timing considerations, location, involving the media, marketing strategies, and procedures for registration, as well as associated amenities. The administrator may be responsible for the majority of the planning process depending upon the size of the organization. However, other approaches to planning is encouraged such as using advisory committees and councils, staff, and other committed and interested groups of individuals.

Organizing and Structuring

The functions of organizing and structuring is the heart of the program development process. It is here that close attention is paid to the organizational development and structure of the program elements and intended outcomes. Who will be responsible for particular components of the program? What content and curriculum must be developed? How will the learning activities be selected? Who will be responsible for conducting the classes, registering students, ordering books, printing brochures, reserving classroom space, ordering learning materials, evaluating the program, learner, and instructor, and so forth. The development of checklists and *Gantt charts* (a means of identifying tasks and indicating their duration based on a time scale) are valuable methods as you engage in organizing, structuring, and implementing the specifics of your program planning process.

Leading

Leadership is an important function for adult, community, and continuing education administrators, unfortunately not all administrators are leaders. Leadership is a process "that helps direct and mobilize people and/or their ideas. . . . leadership does not produce consistency and order. . . . it produces movement" (Kotter, 1990, pp. 3–4). Edelson (1992) would suggest this is the "new leadership" which is grounded within the newer paradigm of the learning organization. Leadership from his perspective is less hierarchical and more decentralized, team-oriented, and empowering. Knox (1991) states, "Effective administrators are leaders who achieve results with and through other people" (p. 222). As an administrator how does this occur?

Kotter (1990) suggests that this happens by:

1. establishing direction—developing a vision of the future . . . along with strategies for producing the changes needed to achieve that vision

2. aligning people—communicating the direction to those whose cooperation may be needed so as to create coalitions that understand the vision and that are committed to its achievement

3. motivating and inspiring—keeping people moving in the right direction despite major political, bureaucratic, and resource barriers to change by appealing to vary basic, but often untapped, human needs, values, and emotions.

Administrators who exemplify leadership in this manner are providing coherence to the program development process and lending support to the development of a learning organization.

Staffing

Another essential function of the administrator is selecting and developing staff. Staff can include paid as well as volunteer positions within the organization. They could be support personnel, instructors, tutors, program coordinators, instructional designers, etc. Is there a process for selecting staff which includes avenues for announcing open positions, procedures for conducting the interview, descriptions of each position, a process for offering the position to a candidate, and procedures for evaluating staff performance against established standards and expectations? Does the parent organization, program, or agency have written policies and procedures that govern and explain necessary information for associated personnel? Selecting appropriate staff to fulfill the various positions associated with the organization or program is a demanding responsibility. Careful consideration of staff selection is warranted. Considering the preponderance of part-time instructors and volunteers associated with adult, community, and continuing education programs, it is even more essential that serious deliberations be taken when matching the individual's skills with the assigned duties.

Staff development is another element of the staffing function. Is an orientation program available? Does the organization or program provide staff in-service training or workshops to enhance their understanding and performance of their roles? Does the administrator encourage development through attending professional meetings and conferences? Sharing informative articles from journals and magazines? Schedule time with staff personnel concerning their insights and concerns? While administrators are concerned with managerial tasks and functions, they should also be, above all, a continuing educator to staff.

Budgeting

The administrator's ability to manage financial matters of the organization or program is an essential function. Ericksen (1993) states that the most valuable quantitative tool available to an administrator is the budget, because after its development "it can be used to manage and control the future financial activity of the organization" (p. 39). Budgeting is such a crucial function to any organization because it "coordinates and harmonizes the utilization of scarce financial resources by comparing actual results against expected outcomes" (p. 39). Effective administrators understand various types of budgets and are able to utilize financial tools that enhance the program development process. Financial resources and support have become more difficult for adult, community, and continuing education organizations to secure in recent years. It is even more imperative that administrators become more accountable, creative, flexible, and future-oriented in the management and control of the budgeting function.

Marketing

The success and effectiveness of adult, community, and continuing education programs depends to a large extent on marketing efforts. Administrators must be grounded in the concepts, principles, and implementation strategies associated with marketing and public relations. Marketing is a complex process with diverse elements. As an administrator it is essential to be educated in the design and development of a marketing plan, promotional strategies for marketing programs, cost-effective direct-mail marketing, as well as how to develop effective brochures, flyers, and use other techniques that generate increased participation. Public relations is part of the marketing process in which the administrator promotes the image and goodwill of the organization or program. The administrator is heavily involved in the development of a public relations plan as well as aware of strategies to achieve the plan. Marketing and public relations are indispensable functions that the administrator must recognize as critical to the position.

Evaluation

Administrators engage in evaluative processes for an array of purposes such as accountability and justification to the sponsoring organization, determining how well program objectives were achieved, making decisions related to program improvement, providing feedback to program participants and instructors, to recognize components throughout the program development process that were not successful, to assess social impact upon the community, or to describe program outcomes to other educators. There are an array of evaluation types. Do you want to evaluate the program or organization, the learners, the instructors, or the staff? Administrators must be able to select the most appropriate type of evaluation and the methods that will be employed. While much is written about evaluation and its importance, it is less clear as to how administrators utilize and implement the results in their own practices to improve program planning. Evaluation is an administrative function that entails measurement and appraisal or judgments. Honest and ethical processes must be incorporated into this evaluative function if informed and useful outcomes are expected.

In summary, these nine functions are essential elements of effective adult, community, and continuing education administration. The degree of intensity, involvement, and utility of these functions by administrators certainly depends upon the type of role they possess and the size of the organization.

Skills

Certain skills are needed to be an effective and efficient administrator while operating and carrying out administrative functions. A brief discussion of some of these essential skills follows.

Understanding Perspective and Purpose

Effective administrators have a historical perspective about adult, community, and continuing education and understand the multitude of purposes. Reading the literature can provide administrators with an appropriate perspective and assist them in recognizing the influences that major trends and philosophical issues have had upon society over the years. The ability to place them in proper context allows the administrator to articulate clearly the program or agency mission and its relationship to goal and objective setting and how such action helps achieve societal, institutional, and learner needs (Knox, 1990).

Knowing Communities

Administrators need to understand that they operate in a multitude of communities that are connected by cultural, social, psychological, economic, political, environmental, and technological elements (Galbraith, 1990a, 1992). While geographical communities, those communities having locality relevance and whereby people within the community have local access to a diversity of activities that are necessary in day-to-day living, may most often define and influence the administrative functions carried out by the agency or program, there are other communities that are essential as well. There are communities of interest and communities of function. Galbraith (1992) states that communities of interest "are those groups of individuals bound by some single common interest or set of common interests" (p. 9) such as leisure interests, civic and special political interests, or religious interests. Galbraith continues by suggesting that "Communities of function are those groups identified by the function of major life roles such as teacher, attorney, doctor, farmer, student, homemaker, parent, and so forth" (p. 9). Understanding the diversity of communities that exist will positively influence how programs are planned and operated as well as how marketing and public relations efforts are carried out.

Communicating and Coordinating

Essential to any administrator is the ability to utilize written, oral, and nonverbal communication effectively. The everyday tasks of writing memos, reports, communicating with staff, peers, colleagues, and outside agency and program personnel, for example, demands effective written and oral communication. Effective communication influences coordinating efforts within the program as well as maintaining cooperation, networking, and advocacy efforts with external agencies. Such qualities influence the responsiveness and versatility you have in dealing with diverse groups and how effectively conflicts are resolved. Good communication and coordinating skills provide a foundation for many of the administrative functions such as mission and philosophy, staffing, leading, marketing, organizing and structuring, planning, and evaluation.

Programming

Understanding program development processes is another essential skill for the administrator. Knox (1990) suggests that program development is comprised of analyzing program context and needs, collaborating with instructors in setting objectives, selecting and organizing learning activities, and evaluating program worth. In coordination with this process, administrators are assisting instructors in making judgments about the program based on the data, objectives and standards. Guglielmino, Frock, and Burrichter (1988) suggest that collaborative skills are an essential quality of a successful administrator. In addition, within the programming skill area is the notion of understanding the adult as a learner. It is the responsibility of the administrator to understand the adult development process and life roles of adults and how they influence marketing, counseling, and instruction. If effective instruction is to occur, administrators must assist program instructors to understand adults as learners. This may include participation rates, shifting personalities and needs, and learning styles.

Courtenay (1993) cites several elements that are unique to adult, community, and continuing education programming efforts. Since the majority of these programs are nonprofit in nature, administrators must possess the skills to develop programs that are a secondary function within a larger organization. This marginality status affects the leading as well as the program evaluation functions of the administrator. A second element is the consequence of "part-timism" in which the majority of learners, instructors, and volunteers are not full time, thus affecting the staffing, and leading functions. As Courtenay (1993) states, "the manager of a smaller unit having mostly part-time staff has the added burden of creatively motivating instructors—who view their job as a secondary priority in their professional life—to accept the importance of and to participate in staff development activities" (p. 14). Understanding the unique aspects of programming is a critical skill for the administrator and perhaps the most important one to possess.

Working with Groups

Another skill that is imperative for the administrator is to work effectively with groups. Working with groups provides a means of building strong and viable adult, community, and continuing education programs, expanding services, and strengthening community ties. Utilizing various kinds of groups is key in enhancing and improving planning efforts, conserving resources, increasing outreach efforts, as well as opportunities to work with diverse populations. Charuhas (1993) states that "the ability of administrators to work with groups in a constructive and wholly integrated manner will result in increased communication, enhanced understanding of their community, and improved programming" (p. 46). Administrators may form focus groups, task forces, and advisory committees to access needed information such as changing demographics, economics, politics, and attitudes of a community toward the agency or program. Such information could, for example, affect the future goals, objective setting, planning, organizing and structuring, staffing, and budgeting functions of the administrator. In addition, administrators may engage in coalitions, cooperatives, and alliances external to the administrator's program or agency. These types of groups work together because they have a "mutual interest or need to achieve a common goal or solve a common problem" (p. 49). Administrators may also find legal, fiscal, and contractual requirements have forced them into subcontracts, partnerships, planning councils, and other self-regulatory groups that resulted from mandated coordination of services as stipulated by funding sources or a contractual arrangement among agencies. Working with any group, the administrator must be involved as a facilitator and participate as well as utilize communication, cooperation, coordination, negotiation, and political skills.

Utilizing Technology

The ability to access, use, and evaluate information through technology is an essential skill for the adult, community, and continuing education administrator. Porter (1993) suggests that administrative functions such as planning, directing, organizing, staffing, and evaluating "can be refined and enhanced through appropriate technologies" (p. 70). Porter provides three sets of technology applications that should be of particular interest to the administrator: computer-based communications, management information system (MIS) technology, and desktop application software. For example, computer-based communications provides access to electronic research databases such as ERIC, e-mail, on-line file sharing, and local area network (LAN)—reporting, or on-line access to professional development budgets and resources. MIS technology provides strategic planning data, sharing and access of policy information, program performance or demographic data, personnel policies and procedures on line, or access to learner performance and learner satisfaction data. Desktop applications software allows for spreadsheets and other simple forms of program budgeting, mapping, computer assisted design, file sharing tools, individual and group scheduling, project planning software, desktop publishing, statistical tools, group development activities, and project accounting.

Acquiring and utilizing technology makes information more directly and readily available which will produce "increased access to administrative data, improved information sharing, decentralized information management and decision-making, curricular changes and enhancements, and remote access to research information" (Porter, 1993, pp. 74–75). Introducing administrative technology requires careful planning, training, and participation of all who will be involved with its utilization. Administrators can enhance the various functions of their practice by engaging in the use of technology.

Being a Critical Thinker

Effective administrators encourage people around them to take risks, to challenge assumptions, to question, and to consider alternative actions. Agency and program activities will be enhanced when administrators create environments that foster critical thinking; however, to realize this the administrator must lead by example. Jones (1994) describes aspects of the critical thinking process that are appropriate for the administrator:

- Provide the opportunity for people to consider the strengths and weaknesses of opposing points of view.
- Provide opportunities to reflect on, discuss, and evaluate people's beliefs and actions.
- Evaluate a wide range of alternatives when making decisions.
- Encourage adults to raise ethical questions about consequences of actions and decisions of themselves and others.
- Provide a collaborative environment for inquiry.
- Ask probing questions.
- Engage in exploratory dialogue proposing ideas and translating subject matter, insights, and evidence into reflective thought.
- Discuss contradictions in thoughts, words, and actions.
- Encourage the discussion of implications of actions being considered.

Administrators who foster and encourage "thinking time" into their practice and organization will discover a more conducive and productive environment for carrying out adult, community, and continuing education activities.

SUMMARY

This chapter has examined the various aspects of being an administrator in adult, community, and continuing education. It has invited the reader to complete a self-assessment inventory about the functions and skills of being an administrator and to determine the importance of each function and skill in their particular administrative role. A brief description of the multitude of settings or contexts in which administration takes place was presented as well as an examination of important characteristics, functions, and essential skills. With the understanding of being an administrator, we now focus on the various approaches to administration.

APPENDIX A

Self-Assessment Inventory
for Adminstrators of Adult,
Community, and Continuing Education

	Current Proficiency Level					Degree of Importance to My Work				
	Very High 1	High 2	Med 3	Low 4	Very Low 5	Very Low 1	Low 2	Med 3	High 4	Very High 5
APPROACHES TO ADMINISTRATION										
Understanding of a variety of administrative approaches										
Ability to select appropriate concepts and practices for your own organization										
Ability to develop an administrative approach which allows for continuous adaptation to change										
Understanding of the increasing importance of participation and collaboration										
DETERMINING PROGRAM CONTENT										
Understanding of the value of collaborative program development process										
Understanding of the essential elements of a need and interest assessment										
Ability to design an effective need and interest assessment										
Ability to prioritize individual, organizational, and community needs and interests										

Ability to develop appropriate program objectives											
Ability to design educational offerings											
BUDGETING AND FINANCING											
Understanding of the purposes of budgets											
Understanding of the types of budgets											
Understanding of the different approaches to budgeting											
Ability to develop successful budgets											
Understanding of the financial base of the organization											
Knowledge of available supplementary funding sources											
SELECTING AND DEVELOPING STAFF											
Ability to define job roles and responsibilities											
Understanding of the essential components of the staff selection process											
Ability to design and conduct effective interviews											
Understanding of a variety of approaches to staff development											
Understanding of the components of a professional development plan											

	Current Proficiency Level					Degree of Importance to My Work				
	Very High 1	High 2	Med 3	Low 4	Very Low 5	Very Low 1	Low 2	Med 3	High 4	Very High 5
MARKETING AND PUBLIC RELATIONS										
Understanding the differences between marketing and public relations										
Understanding of the elements of a marketing mission										
Ability to develop a marketing plan										
Understanding of effective marketing techniques										
Ability to design an effective public relations plan										
EVALUATION PROGRAMS										
Understanding of formative evaluations										
Understanding of summative evaluations										
Ability to design and conduct evaluations										
Ability to interpret and use evaluation results										
LEGAL AND ETHICAL CONSIDERATIONS										
Understanding of the Affirmative Action and Equal Employment Opportunity guidelines										

Understanding of the pitfalls associated with employment applications and the interview process								
Understanding of the legal issues in the interview process								
Understanding of the Americans with Disabilities Act								
Understanding of contract use, types, and contents								
Ability to recognize ethical dilemmas								
Ability to make ethical decisions								
MAINTAINING EFFECTIVENESS AS AN ADMINISTRATOR								
Understanding of the basic elements for self development and growth								
Understanding of the theory and techniques for creating a learning organization								
Ability to prepare and use professional development plans								
Understanding of essential administration literature resources								

NOTE: To assist in prioritizing your learning needs, multiply your rating for Current Proficiency Level by your rating for Degree of Importance to My Work. Scores of 16 or higher indicate areas in which your greatest learning needs exist.

CHAPTER 2

Approaches to Administration

Although the concept of administration and, certainly, its practice have been evidenced throughout human history, little attention was given to the distillation of principles or guidelines for administrative behavior until the 1800s. The commonly held viewpoint was that the administration of an enterprise was inextricably linked to the enterprise itself. However, there has been a growing realization that certain concepts and principles of administration are generic.

One of the earliest publications to promote this concept was Woodrow Wilson's essay entitled "The Study of Administration" in 1887. In it, he advocated formal study of administration leading to the development of stable principles and thus reducing the confusion and costliness of what at that time amounted to a trial and error approach to administration (Owens, 1991).

Since that time, increasing attention has been given to the emerging fields of study variously referred to as administration, management, and the addition of the separate but related concept of leadership. Despite some differences in the naming of the various stages of thought and practice, there has been a recognizable evolution in those concepts over the years (Hellreigel & Slocum, 1992; Kowalski, 1988; Moorhead & Griffin, 1989; Owens, 1991). The earliest focus was on task and structure, establishing the basis for what has come to be known as classical organizational theory, or the traditional approach to management. Growing out of an engineering model, the classical approach attempted to organize and systematize human behavior in organizations on a mechanistic model. The emphasis on the classical approach was followed, not surprisingly, by a swing of the pendulum to a concentration on the human factors in production and efficiency, usually referred to as the human relations movement. These two movements formed the basis for the two major theoretical approaches to management which persist to this day. Three contemporary perspectives, all with their roots in the second half of the 1900s, also offer important insights into approaches to the administration of adult, community, and continuing education: the organizational behavior movement, the contingency approach, and the systems approach.

Following a brief presentation of these five administrative approaches, the selection of an appropriate administrative stance for adult, community, and continuing education will be discussed. The emphasis will be on an integrative approach which incorporates valuable concepts and practices from each of the five administrative perspectives and allows for continuous adaptation to change.

PRIMARY ADMINISTRATIVE PERSPECTIVES

The major elements of the five primary approaches to administration are depicted in Figure 2.1. While a detailed discussion of each approach is beyond the scope of this book, they will be described briefly.

The Classical Approach

Emerging in the late 1890s through the early 1900s, the classical or traditional approach can be subdivided into three main branches: scientific management, beureaucratic management, and administrative management. While each branch had a slightly different emphasis, all were based on a mechanistic model and were designed to make organizations run "like well-oiled machines" (Hellreigel & Slocum, 1992).

Scientific Management

Three names are preeminent in the scientific management branch of classical organizational theory: Frederick Taylor, the Gilbreths, and Henry Gantt. Coming from a career as an engineer in the steel industry in the late 1800s, Frederick Taylor (1911) became one of the top engineering consultants in American industry in the early 1900s. The Industrial Revolution spurred the development of Taylor's "principles of scientific management," which focused on two major areas: the clear delineation of areas of responsibility of management and workers and the application of a mechanistic model to workers which encompassed their selection, training, and the manner in which they were expected to perform their work. His principles established management as the brains of the organization and workers as the brawn, asserting the need for a strict division of responsibility between management and workers, with man-

ADMINISTRATIVE PERSPECTIVES	MAJOR FOCUS / TENENTS	MAJOR FIGURES
CLASSICAL	• maximum efficiency in task completion • structural & organizational issues • division of responsibility • Theory X view of workers	• Frederick Taylor • Frank & Lillian Gilbreth • Max Weber • Henri Fayoul
HUMAN RELATIONS	• social, psychological factors • group interactions • Theory Y view of workers	• Elton Mayo • Abraham Maslow • Mary Parker Follett • Kurt Lewin • Robert Bales
ORGANIZATION BEHAVIOR	• interaction of individual and organization	• Chester Barnard • Jacob Getzels • Egon Guba
CONTINGENCY	• recognition that there is no one best approach • flexibility, adaptability	• Joan Woodward • Ken Blanchard • Paul Hersey
SYSTEMS APPROACH	• recognition that any organization is a series of interacting systems operating within a wider system	• Ludwig Von Bertalannffy • Peter Senge • Karen Watkins • Victoria Marsick

Figure 2.1 Five administrative perspectives

agers setting goals and objectives, planning, and supervising, while workers completed the tasks assigned to them exactly as they were trained to complete them. Taylor's principles also led to the development of specific, scientifically designed, sequential processes for the accomplishment of job tasks with maximum efficiency.

Frank and Lillian Gilbreth expanded upon Taylor's approach, using motion pictures to analyze the steps involved in a task and determine ways to restructure it for greater efficiency. So enthusiastic were they about the value of the time and motion studies that they even applied them in their home, giving their 12 children lessons on the most efficient way to take a shower and requiring them to study vocabulary words posted on the wall during "periods of unavoidable delay" in the bathroom (Gilbreth, 1948). The techniques used by the Gilbreths and Taylor are the basis for job redesign techniques used in industry today. Lillian

Gilbreth, who carried on their work after Frank's death, added a focus on the human side of industrial engineering, calling for standard working hours with scheduled breaks and lunch hours, a safe working environment, and protection of children from exploitation in the workplace (Hellreigel & Slocum, 1992).

Henry Gantt, an associate of Taylor, is famous for his Gantt charts, which are still widely used today. They visually depict various stages of a project and include deadlines for the completion of each stage. Quota systems and bonuses for workers exceeding their quotas are also ascribed to Gantt (Hellreigel & Slocum, 1992).

Bureaucratic Management

Bureaucratic management, as proposed by Max Weber (1947), focuses on the overall organizational structure, attempting to provide a logical blueprint of the way an organization should function to ensure efficiency, fairness, and predictability. Major principles of this approach include division of labor based on specialization and personal expertise, a comprehensive system of rules which provide guidelines for the behavior of employees, a clearly defined hierarchy which ranks jobs according to power and authority and delineates reporting relationships, and impersonality (the minimization of personal and emotional factors in the workplace, leading to the requirement that rules and standards form the basis for hiring, evaluation, and promotion). Weber saw this approach as one means of reducing the impact of authoritarian industrialists and long-standing class systems and political systems, but he also recognized and warned against the dangers of the proliferation of bureaucracy beyond a workable level. His bureaucratic approach is still used very effectively by companies in which many routine tasks need to be performed within specified timelines and with a high degree of accuracy.

Administrative Management

Henri Fayoul (1949), a French industrialist, focused on the manager as the key to increased efficiency and productivity rather than on the worker or the organization as a whole. The first to group managerial functions into the now standard categories of planning, organizing, leading, and controlling, he developed fourteen principles which should govern the management process and advocated that managers be trained in applying these principles. Some of his principles echo concepts of scientific or bureaucratic management, such as division of labor, authority of managers, discipline (respect of rules and agreements governing the organization), and subordination of individual interest to the common goal. Others introduce new concepts, such as unity of command (employees receive instructions about a particular function from only one person), unity of direction (employees working on a project should be coordinated and directed by one manager), and the scalar chain, or scalar principle (one uninterrupted line of authority should be traceable from the highest to the lowest levels of the organization).

While there were strengths and weaknesses in each of these approaches and some of the concepts and principles are still used effectively in some types of companies today, the appropriateness of their application in educational settings was and is questionable. Some argued that the factory model was not applicable to education, but others embraced the concepts wholeheartedly. Even Elwood Cubberly (1916), one of the most influential educators in the early 1900s, became caught up in the industrial focus of the period and described schools as "factories in which the raw materials are to be shaped . . . into products to meet the various demands of life" (p. 337). Owens (1991) points out that professors of educational administration, enamored by the principles of scientific management, did detailed studies of the tasks of various educational administrators. Based on a study which revealed that the supervision of janitors was one responsibility of superintendents, research was conducted to determine the most effective means of completing janitorial tasks such as mopping, sweeping, or waxing floors, and some preparation programs for superintendents actually included a study of these techniques to ensure that they could properly train and supervise their employees. As more and more problems became evident in this factory-based, task and structure-focused approach to administration that ignored the needs of the worker for recognition, interpersonal interaction, and some measure of job satisfaction, a new focus began to emerge.

The Human Relations Approach

Several important forces converged in the 1920s and 1930s to usher in an approach to management which recognized the importance of the human factors in the workplace. In reaction to the abuses of the early industrial era, workers were beginning to band together to demand reasonable pay and working conditions. Solid research demonstrated that determining the most efficient way to do the work was not sufficient to ensure maximum productivity, and a number of influential authors contributed to the understanding of the social and interactional aspects of administration.

The Rise of Labor Unions

The formation of labor unions, with their demands for fair pay and benefits, regular and reasonable working hours, and improved working conditions focused attention on the worker as a person rather than as one more aspect of the workplace to be manipulated at will. Together, the unskilled workers had a voice which could not be ignored, and salaries, benefits, and working conditions began to improve. The unions' power was solidified and increased by 1930s legislation which prohibited management from limiting union activities and legalized collective bargaining. The efforts of the workers to make their needs known through the unions were supplemented by the surprising findings of research strongly grounded in the scientific management approach.

The Hawthorne Experiments

Concurrently with the rise of the labor unions, a series of experiments was being conducted by the National Research Council at the Western Electric plant in Hawthorne, Illinois. The initial experiment, designed to determine the ideal level of lighting for maximum productivity, instead revealed that productivity rose in both the experimental and control groups. In the experimental group, positive gains were noted not only at what experts considered to be the optimum level of illumination, but also when the lighting was reduced to a near-twilight level. This finding, verified by further research, led to the conclusion that has come to be called the *Hawthorne effect*: When workers are given special attention, their performance is likely to improve regardless of working conditions (Mayo, 1945). The Hawthorne studies established the impact of psychological and social factors on human productivity.

Authors Focusing on Social and Psychological Factors in Productivity

A third major influence on the introduction of humanistic concerns into management theory and practice was the writings of thinkers such as Abraham Maslow and Mary Parker Follett (Metcalf & Urwick, 1942). Maslow presented his theory that human motivation arises from a hierarchical series of needs, with the higher needs unable or unlikely to be addressed until the lower needs, such as health and safety, were addressed. This theory, which provided major insights into the variety of factors involved in human motivation, became well known and widely accepted.

Follett greatly enlarged the understanding of management when she described it as a social process which was inextricably linked to and affected by its context. Her views not only ushered in the human relations movement, but also pioneered some of the concepts integral to what is now called the contingency approach to leadership (Owens, 1991). In fact, she proposed concepts that are among those being voiced and implemented today by the most admired organizations: reduction of hierarchies, the use of teams, participative management based on the belief that there is much to be learned from the individual who is actually doing the work, cooperative conflict resolution, and the belief that leadership is based on ability, not position in a hierarchy (Linden, 1995).

Other major contributions during this period included Jacob Moreno's sociometric analysis, used to determine the informal structure of groups, and Robert Bales' interaction analysis, which revealed two major dimensions of the behavior of successful groups: task orientation and the maintenance of productive human relations. Kurt Lewin's (1951) studies of group decision making also provided important insights during this period.

Although his work appeared long after the initiation of the human relations movement, Douglas McGregor (1960) created the most memorable comparison of the classical and human relations approaches when he described the assumptions of Theory X and Theory Y managers. Theory X assumptions, which are generally associated with managers using the classical approach, present humans as basically lazy and lacking in ambition. Their primary behaviors are to seek security while avoiding work and responsibility. Based on these assumptions, the manager must control, direct, coerce, and even threaten employees if the necessary work is to be completed. In contrast, Theory Y assumptions present humans as internally motivated beings who view work as a natural part of their lives. Under favorable conditions, they seek responsibility, are committed to goals, and are innovative. These assumptions are more congruent with the human relations approach, and managers who accept them are more likely to view their role as facilitative and collaborative rather than directive.

The Organizational Behavior Perspective

The organizational behavior movement broadened the focus of administrative concerns and moved toward synthesis, emphasizing the need to study not only human behavior in organizations or the organization itself, but also to examine the interface between human behavior and the organization in order to attain a comprehensive understanding of organizational behavior (Moorhead & Griffin, 1989). This interface has two aspects: the interaction between the individual and the organization and the interaction between the informal organization and the formal organization.

Chester Barnard (1938) was one of the earliest authors to emphasize the need for understanding the relationship between the formal, or official organization, and the informal organization and to consider the interaction between the needs and goals of the workers and those of the organization. In *The Functions of the Executive*, he described the organization as a social system and presented his acceptance theory of authority, which was in direct contrast to the bureaucratic concept of top-down management. In the acceptance theory perspective, authority is viewed as originating in the individual who can choose whether to follow a directive from an administrator or not. Some of the factors involved in that decision might be the level of understanding of what is expected, the ability to carry it out, or the degree to which it is consistent with personal values. The task of the administrator then becomes more complex; for an organization to function maximally, the needs and expectations of the workers must be considered as well as the needs and purposes of the organization. One of the better-known depictions of this concept is the Getzels-Guba (1957) model of the organization as a social system, which represents the organizational dimension (institution, role, expectation) interacting with the personal dimension (individual, personality, need-disposition) to produce observed behavior.

Throughout the 1950s and 1960s, a steady stream of research and theory dealt with issues related to the interaction of formal and informal organizations and individual and organizational needs and expectations. A wide variety of disciplines contributed to this line of research: psychology and social psychology, management, sociology, anthropology, and political science (Owens, 1991).

The Contingency Approach

Much of the early research in the areas of administration and management was devoted to the attempt to discover universal solutions to problems within organizations. Certainly, the addition of human factors, and the interaction of human factors and organizational structures, to the areas of focus within studies of administration led to new insights and resulted in substantial progress toward a better understanding of organizational functioning, but the natural tendency to discover the best approach remained strong. In the 1960s Joan Woodward (1980) studied

100 English firms in an attempt to identify the management principles adhered to by the most successful companies. Her research revealed no one best approach for all companies, but did reveal an interesting relationship. Companies that were involved in mass production were more effective under bureaucratic management. Based on this research and other new insights, theorists began to generalize, concluding that organizations involved in performing routine tasks in fairly predictable environments could normally benefit from classical, bureaucratic structures, while those that operate in an environment of change which requires adaptation and quick response are more likely to be successful in a less bureaucratic organization. Teamwork, collaboration, and integration become their tools for responding to change.

While these generalizations were somewhat helpful, it soon became apparent that there were a number of other contingencies besides type of task and stability of the environment that impacted the effectiveness of an organizational structure. Among these are the goals of the organization, the type of technology involved, and the composition of the workforce. In the contingency approach, an appropriate organizational structure and management approach would be chosen on the basis of an examination of these factors. Perhaps the best-known statement of the considerations of a contingency-based approach is Hersey and Blanchard's (1982) situational leadership.

The advent of the contingency approach underlined the fact that there is no one right answer to administrative issues. What works under one set of circumstances or in one particular setting does not necessarily work in a similar setting or even in the same setting. Despite our attempts to order our world and make it predictable, the complexities of organizations and the humans who interact with them and within them make universal solutions improbable. This realization called into question the long-standing practice of uncritically applying management approaches developed in business and industry to the very different setting of education and concurrently paved the way for an even broader analysis of the internal and external factors that affect the functioning of an organization. This analysis is cental to what has come to be called the systems approach.

The Systems Approach

The systems approach to management looks at the organization as an association of interrelated and interdependent parts working together to meet the goals of the organization. Systems theory was introduced by a biologist, Ludwig von Bertalannffy (1950), who used the analogy of a living organism to illustrate a system in which each part of the whole affects the other parts. He went on to point out that an organism is an *open system*, in that it exists as a part of a larger system which it affects and is affected by. Bounds, Dobbins, and Fowler (1995) point out the contrast between this concept with the mechanistic view of the classical approach, which focuses on internal designs without considering relationships with the environment.

The systems approach is usually conceptualized as a series of inputs acted upon by a transformation process which results in certain outputs. A feedback loop allows for needed adjustments to ensure that the desired outputs are achieved. In the open systems model, this process is seen as taking place within the larger environment, which may produce additional inputs at any time. Figure 2.2 illustrates the concept. An essential tenet of the systems approach is the recognition of the layering of systems operating within other systems. Figure 2.3 illustrates some of the interacting systems within and external to a continuing higher education unit. Figure 2.4 does the same for an adult/community education organization and then breaks out some of the interacting units within the system in more detail.

Because of the emphasis on interactions within the systems approach, both the organizational schema and the importance of each of the elements within the system become easily recognizable. Internally, the focus on interdependence can lead to greater understanding of the tasks and responsibilities of other units within the organization and greater consideration of the impact of decisions and actions on other units, resulting in a more unified organizational effort. The recognition of interdependence with the external environment inherent in the open systems model is essential to the success of the adult, community, and continuing education administrator, who must continually be involved in environmental scanning as part of a comprehensive needs and interest assessment to ensure that program offerings address the needs of the target population. Some prominent authors in the field of management assert that the translation of systems concepts to effective practice in dealing with the human aspects of management is difficult (Hellriegel & Slocum, 1992). Bolman and Deal (1984) point out that even in Katz and Kahn's (1978) presentation of an open systems framework as a basis for examining the social psychology of organizations, human issues such as leadership, motivation, and decision making are not effectively addressed within the concept of the open system. They hypothesize that the problem stems from two sources: differences in terminology and the generality of sys-

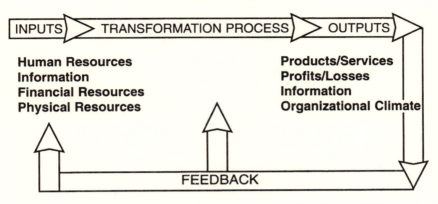

Figure 2.2 Open systems model

tems concepts, which tends to limit their applicability to specific predictions about human systems. In contrast, Bounds, Dobbins, and Fowler (1995), while recognizing that managers have had difficulty in translating open systems theory into managerial action in the past, assert that Total Quality Management (TQM) is an extension of the open systems model in which its full value has become apparent. They present seven principles of TQM which reveal its firm base in open systems theory as well as its incorporation of the best ideas from the approaches already described:

Principle 1: Focus on delivering customer value.
Principle 2: Continuously improve the system and its processes.
Principle 3: Manage processes, not just people.
Principle 4: Look for root causes to solve and prevent problems.
Principle 5: Collect data and use science for analysis.
Principle 6: Remember that people are the organization's primary
                   resource.
Principle 7: Work in teams to execute processes efficiently and effectively.

Senge's (1990) and Watkins and Marsick's (1993) descriptions of the development of *learning organizations* as the only effective approach for managing in the midst of unprecedented rates of change are firmly grounded in the systems approach. They provide invaluable guidelines for the creation of an organization in which work and learning are integrally related and continuous growth and renewal to meet ever-changing needs are an accepted expectation.

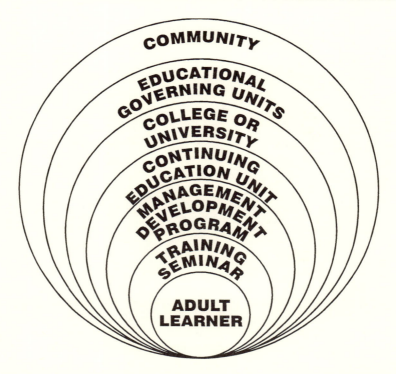

Figure 2.3 Some interacting systems within and external to a continuing higher education program

SELECTING AN APPROPRIATE
ADMINISTRATIVE STANCE

In an adult, community, or continuing education unit or any other organizational entity, the wise educational leader will recognize the value of using workable concepts from a variety of approaches. Whether this is operationalized as situational leadership, as eclecticism, or within the more comprehensive framework of TQM or the concept of the learning organization is not as important as recognizing that educational institutions are complex organizations incorporating many different types of tasks which may require different types of approaches.

From the classical approach, effective ways of handling the tasks which are routine and repetitive can be gleaned. Functions such as registration, building maintenance, and implementation of employee benefit

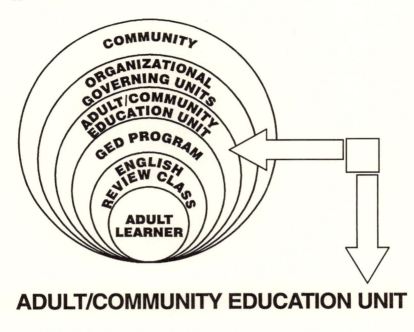

ADULT/COMMUNITY EDUCATION UNIT

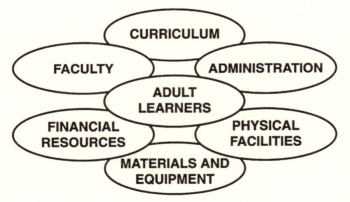

Figure 2.4 Interacting systems external to and within an adult/community education program

programs can be expeditiously handled by using some of the principles of scientific management and bureaucratic organization (but not to the exclusion of consideration of the human factor). However, the central task of an educational organization is highly creative and nonroutine, requiring a very different approach. The art of facilitating learning, in which the human factors are the major consideration, both in working with the learners and in the administrators' dealings with the learning facilitators, requires the insight into social and psychological factors and individual and group interaction gained from the human relations movement. The lessons of the organizational behavior approach and the contingency approach are also important for the adult, community, and continuing education administrator. The interaction of individual and organizational needs, goals, and expectations cannot be ignored if the organization is to achieve its potential, and the understanding that there is no one right approach that will work in every set of circumstances provides a basis for the flexibility and reflection which characterize effective educational administration.

Finally, the concepts of the systems approach are unquestionably valuable for adult, community, and continuing educators. By purpose and philosophy, they are integrally involved with the individuals and communities which constitute their target population. Understanding of the interacting systems within the organization as well as the interaction of the educational organization with the wider community is essential, especially in a rapidly changing environment. In dealing with complex educational organizations which must be closely linked to the individuals and communities which they serve, it is essential to remember three major points:

- All parts of the system are important.
- They all impact each other and are impacted by external forces.
- They all interact to create the image and the actuality of the institution.

These systems concepts facilitate a view of the organization as a dynamic unit as well as an understanding of the need for the organization to respond to internal and external changes in order to maintain effectiveness.

In a time of rapid change and the proliferation of educational opportunities for adults, educational administrators must be acutely aware of and responsive to change in the community, in the population of learners and in their needs, and within their own organizations or institutions. Technology is expanding so rapidly that all of the technology available in 1991 is expected to represent only one percent of the available technology in the year 2050 (Cetron & Davis, 1991); individuals are changing jobs and even careers more often and are experiencing more change even if they stay within the same jobs (Cetron, Gayle, & Soriano, 1985); and the traditional majority population will soon become the minority (Boyett & Conn, 1991). The implications of these and a myriad of other changes present new challenges for society as a whole, for the individuals who make it up, and, therefore, for adult, community, and continuing education.

The administrators who successfully meet these challenges will be those who are flexible, proactive, and collaborative, involving their organizations and shareholders in an ongoing process of internal and external analysis in order to simultaneously maintain an effective, fully functioning unit while scanning the future and planning for needed changes. Four central elements of an approach to administration are implicit in this statement:

1. a proactive stance which is based on a clear understanding of the organization: its mission, values, goals, strengths, and weaknesses

2. a recognition of the adult, community, and continuing education organization as a system within a system, which implies a continuous cycle of needs assessment and evaluation to determine if individual and community needs are being met

3. use of a collaborative approach which simultaneously taps and develops human resources, both within the organizational system and in relation to other parts of the system

4. a recognition of the constant need for organizational change and renewal, or continuous improvement

These elements suggest the need for a flexible, continuous, collaborative planning structure such as the one proposed by Simerly (1987). He defines strategic planning as a process which incorporates designing, implementing and monitoring plans for improving organizational decision making. Morrison, Renfro, and Boucher (1984) emphasize the difference between strategic planning and long-range or long-term planning, pointing out that long-range planning normally focuses on currently identified issues and problems, while strategic planning targets potential opportunities. This difference in emphasis is a vital one for the adult, community, and continuing education administrator because it broadens the focus of planning and incorporates the certainty of change.

Simerly (1987) asserts that strategic planning is most effective when it includes seven essential activities: conducting a management audit, clarifying organizational values, creating a mission statement, establishing goals and objectives, creating an action plan, conducting a reality test, and designing a feedback system. Morrison, Renfro, and Boucher (1984) offer a similar list, but with greater emphasis on the use of environmental scanning to stay abreast of new trends and developments.

A strategic planning structure allows the organization to stay focused on plans, yet be flexible and adaptive and, therefore, able to deal with change effectively. Figure 2.5 outlines what such a structure might look like. As is reflected in the figure, it is essential that the initial and ongoing development of the strategic plan involve individuals from all levels of the organization as well as representatives of the target population to be served. Kanter, Stein, and Jick (1992) point out that building and maintaining success in a period of continuing change is only possible when the entire organization participates. Even in business and industry, where the top-down, hierarchical approach to management was developed to extreme levels, the emphasis now has changed to cooperative, participative approaches. Elimination of hierarchies, use of self-directed teams and shared decision making are now common among the most successful companies (Guglielmino & Guglielmino, 1994; Ray & Rinzler, 1993); and the new focus on employee participation and development at all levels of the organization mirrors the adult education mission of facilitating individual growth and development for all adults.

Senge (1990), in fact, calls for the conversion of all organizations to learning organizations, in which employees at all levels are continuously learning and collaborating in order to continue to function effectively in an atmosphere of constant change. Interestingly, Senge asserts that most educational organizations are not learning organizations (O'Neil, 1995). Hindered by their traditional bureaucratic structure, they are not well designed to deal with change. Administrators of adult, community, and continuing education must overcome this inherent barrier and develop a flexible, collaborative, administrative approach if they are to meet the challenge of offering appropriate and effective learning opportunities in an atmosphere of constant change.

SUMMARY

Understanding the evolution of approaches to management and administration over the years can provide useful insights to the administrator of adult, community, and continuing education. The classical approach, which focused on task and structure, provided some models for

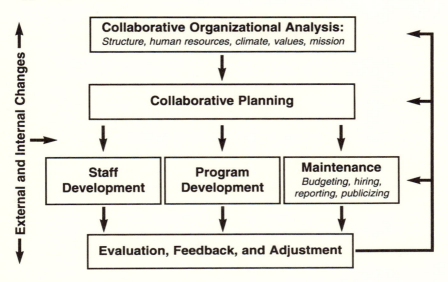

Figure 2.5 Strategic planning structure

organization and systematization which are still used today, particularly in very stable organizations or for specific functions in which the work is largely repetitive and unchanging. The human relations approach emphasized the human dimension, which was generally ignored in the classical period. It was followed by the organizational behavior movement, which attempts to synthesize the focus on task and structure with the human factors and address the interaction between the individual worker and the organization.

The contingency approach emphasizes the uniqueness of each situation and the fact that there is no one right way to address administrative issues across all organizations, and the systems approach provides a means of visualizing the organization as a network of interacting systems operating within a wider system, the external environment.

The chapter concludes with the need for adult, community, and continuing education administrators to be acutely aware of and responsive to change. A collaborative approach based on an understanding of the systems within and external to the organization is recommended, as is the development of a flexible administrative system that is continuously examined and improved.

CHAPTER 3

Determining Program Content

The major point of contact between an adult, community, or continuing education program and the learners it serves is the educational activities it offers. Consequently, careful determination of what will be offered and when and how it will be offered is critical to the success of the organization. This chapter will address the determination of program content as a multistage process, recognizing that it involves decisions and actions related to the program as a whole (macro level) and to the individual educational activities which are a part of that program (micro level). Emphasis will be placed on the macro level, where the program administrator's involvement is greater.

What do learners need, now and in the near future? What do they want? What will they actually enroll in? What will our resources permit us to offer? While in practice we often refer to the attempt to answer these and other related questions as *needs assessment*, the process of determining what learning opportunities will be offered encompasses a much broader spectrum of activities than the technical definition of this term would suggest.

In the professional literature, needs assessment is defined very narrowly, most often being referred to as a discrepancy between a desired condition or state of affairs and the present condition (Knowles, 1980; Nowlen, 1980; Sork & Caffarella, 1989; Witkin, 1984). Following this definition, one is led to view needs assessment solely as the identification of a deficient state. While this approach is familiar and easy to understand, its best use is in programs designed for remediation. The vast majority of adult, community, and continuing education programs, which focus on personal and professional growth and continued development, are better served by a broader definition. In addition, the focus on deficiencies which is inherent in the discrepancy definition can create a dangerous myopia for administrators of adult programs in an era of rapid change, when continual reevaluation and projection of emerging needs is vital.

Perhaps it is time to say what we mean. In this chapter the term *need and interest assessment* (NIA) will be used to refer to the process of gathering information about the needs and interests of the target group as one basis for making decisions about program content. NIA is only one part of the process of determining program content, but it is an extremely vital part.

Figure 3.1 depicts the program development model which provides the basis for the determination of program content as described in this chapter. After an overview of the entire process, the major steps will be discussed in more detail. Special attention will be given to the need and interest assessment.

STEPS IN DETERMINING PROGRAM CONTENT

The determination of program content consciously or unconsciously begins from the central foundation of the education unit: its purpose. Clients served and major programming thrusts are often implicit in the purpose statement. From this base, three major types of information are tapped or developed: current needs and interests of the target population, institutional experience (What courses have been successful in the past? What is working in similar programs?) and community data (the big picture).

The information collected from these three areas is then considered in light of a number of factors which have a major influence on what the final program offerings are. Current goals or priorities of the educational unit or a governing body, funding source, or regulatory agency for the unit can have a major impact. Projected future needs of the individuals, organizations, or of the community as a whole are also an important consideration. The availability of resources is another inevitable screen. Which and how many of the areas of need can be addressed with available or accessible human and material resources? Are there other programs in the area which can meet or are meeting some of the needs? Once all these factors are considered, the identified needs and interests can be prioritized, programming goals stated, and the educational offerings developed and implemented. These offerings may take many forms. Degree or certification programs, special interest courses (academic or nonacademic), workshops, seminars, and community forums are among the most common.

The development of each structured offering reflects what might be referred to as a microcosm of the larger design process. An instructor or design team uses information gathered in the larger process in addition

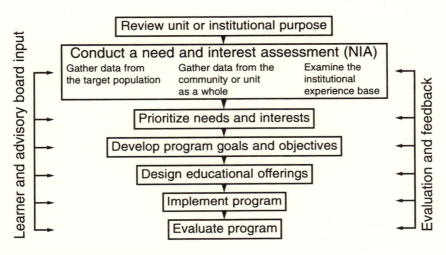

Figure 3.1 Determining program content

to knowledge and experience related to the specific topic and to the selection of appropriate learning strategies, activities, and resources, (content and process expertise) to develop a plan for facilitating learning. This plan may take a number of different forms, depending on the type of offering involved. Among the possibilities are a course outline with detailed lesson plans, a conference or workshop schedule, or a design for a resource center for self-directed learning (Guglielmino & Guglielmino, 1994).

Ideally, learner and community input are incorporated throughout the entire process. An advisory group (or several) made up of learners and other community representatives is usually the most effective and efficient means of obtaining this input.

Notice the integral role that evaluation plays in the process as depicted in the model. Continual reflection on previous steps will provide valuable insights that can influence future actions. Changes in the community, the organization, or the learners may require that previous decisions be revisited. Each of the steps in determining program content will be briefly discussed in the following section.

Review Unit or Institutional Purpose

All programming decisions are made within the framework of the unit's or institution's purpose. A comprehensive review of the purpose will certainly not be necessary every time a programming decision is made. However, in these rapidly changing times, an annual review by a governing board or advisory group is prudent. The purpose and mission of the organization or unit reflect its philosophical base and help determine the target population and content for the NIA.

Conduct a Need and Interest Assessment (NIA)

Despite the fact that participant or target group involvement in the NIA and other aspects of the determination of program content is an important tenet of adult, community, and continuing education, need and interest assessments (NIAs) are often conducted on a very limited basis or omitted entirely in adult, community, and continuing education programs (Kowalski, 1988; Sork & Caffarella, 1989). In *The Modern Practice of Adult Education,* Knowles (1980) reports that in his visits to adult education programs all over the world, he has found that the answer to one question is the best "divining rod" for predicting whether a program will thrive:

> I simply ask on what bases the decisions are made as to what will be offered in the program. If the answer is that the program is entirely planned by the staff on the basis of what the staff thinks people *ought* to be interested in, I can fairly confidently predict that participation in the program will be rather apathetic. On the other hand, if the answer is that the program is planned with the assistance of a planning committee (or advisory council) which conducts periodic surveys of the needs and interests of the clientele the program seeks to serve, then I predict that I will find a thriving program. (p. 82)

Advisory groups are one invaluable source of information for decision making in program planning, but it is often necessary and advisable to gather more precise and quantifiable information from larger or more diverse samples. The recommended use of learner and advisory committee input is sometimes perceived as being difficult to implement. This perception is at least partly attributable to the marked contrast of the involvement approach with the traditional approach. In the traditional approach, which still predominates in the vast majority of institutions, the program is planned by administrators and instructors; learners only become involved when they present themselves to receive the treatment prescribed by the experts (often too late to make any major modifications). Although extra effort is required to obtain learner and community input throughout the NIA, the impact on the program more than justifies that effort.

The benefits of a careful NIA are many:

- The NIA often serves a marketing function, making potential learners more aware of available learning opportunities.
- The very process of assessing needs and interests creates or enhances public perception of the adult, community, or continuing education unit as a responsive, proactive organization.
- The NIA can assist in many important decisions, such as determining placement and timing of offerings and identifying student services requirements for the various sites such as child care or accessibility to public transportation.
- Potential linkages and resources are often discovered, and commitment to the organization is built through the NIA process.
- NIA results provide baseline data that can be used for later evaluation.
- The information gained from an NIA can be used to target later marketing efforts.

If careful attention is not given to the assessment of needs and interests, costly mistakes can easily be made. While we can certainly learn from those mistakes (Sork, 1991), avoiding as many mistakes as possible from the outset seems to be a more advisable approach. When you balance the numerous benefits of NIA with the reported reasons why they are not used more often, it becomes evident that dynamic, growing adult education programs are using NIA, but they have found ways to contain the time, cost, and human resources involved and they use information that is already available whenever possible.

The need and interest assessment for an adult, community, or continuing education program has three major components: gathering data from the population which is expected to participate in the program offerings; gathering data from the community as a whole; and examining the institutional experience base.

Gathering Data from the Target Population

In an effective effort to collect data on needs and interests of potential learners, planning is central. If the entire process is thought through in advance, costly mistakes can be avoided and valuable additional data can be obtained. A suggested sequence of events for a needs and interest assessment includes the following steps:

- Clearly define the purpose of the NIA.
- Identify the target population.
- Determine available resources.
- Choose NIA methods.
- Decide how NIA data will be recorded and analyzed.
- Develop a timeline with responsible parties noted.
- Conduct the NIA.
- Analyze the data.
- Report the results.

Each will be briefly discussed in this chapter, primarily in relation to the first major area of NIA focus, gathering data from the target population. Separate sections will provide additional information about the two other major components of the NIA: gathering data from the community as a whole and examining the institutional experience base.

Define the Purpose of the NIA. A comprehensive NIA may be conducted annually or on a less frequent basis, with more narrowly focused NIAs in the intervening years. External or internal factors may precipitate a targeted NIA; for example, grant funds may become available for a specific group, such as disabled adults, with a requirement for NIA data that you do not currently have. Or, the attendance at a particular group of noncredit courses may be declining, leading you to conduct a special assessment to determine current needs and interests. Other specialized NIAs will probably be conducted on a regular basis, such as the assessment of needs and interests of your own faculty and staff as a basis for designing staff development opportunities. Regardless of its scope, a close examination of the exact purpose of the proposed NIA can save time and money, often revealing ways of combining efforts which conserve resources.

The following questions can be used to clarify the purpose of the NIA and ensure that all parties agree:

- What, exactly, do we hope to accomplish through the proposed NIA?
- Are there other needs for NIA that we can anticipate?
- Can any of these be feasibly combined?

The clear statement of purpose provides the foundation for all the other steps in the NIA.

Identify the Target Population for the NIA. Once the purpose is clearly established, it is usually a simple matter to determine the target population for the NIA. If staff development is the focus, it may be feasible to gather data from and about the entire target population. If the NIA is being used to determine enrichment activities for an entire community, it will usually be necessary to devise some type of sampling technique. Many programs rely heavily on NIA questions added to evaluation forms for current courses. The logic is excellent: the individuals who are currently taking courses or who have taken courses in the past are statistically more likely to enroll in additional classes than a random sample of the population. It is important, however, to supplement this type of data with information from other segments of the population and information on overall community needs in an attempt to more fully address the needs of the entire target population; for example, disabled learners or those in need of basic skills or English as a second language (ESL) classes may constitute an important but previously unserved segment of the population.

Determine Available Resources. What human and material resources are available for conducting the NIA? How much time and money can be dedicated to the effort? Is cooperation with other agencies possible to reduce costs? Can available personnel handle the gathering, compilation, and reporting of data, or will part-time helpers or volunteers be needed? Like the scope of the NIA, costs can range from minimal to major. In some cases, adult, community, and continuing education agencies apply for funding to conduct a major NIA, but most can be managed within the parameters of the annual budget. In a large-scale effort, the costs most likely to require consideration are printing, postage, and payment for consultants or temporary personnel such as survey developers, interviewers, or data analysts.

Choose NIA Methods. A wide range of NIA methods is available for adult programs. Purpose, time, funding, and availability of human resources all contribute to the decision of which methods to use. It is usually wise to seek data through multiple pathways to ensure accuracy.

While it is generally agreed that the survey is the most common method of NIA (Kowalski, 1988; Witkin, 1984), many other methods can produce valuable information. Merriam and Simpson's *Guide to Research for Educators and Trainers of Adults* (1995) provides an excellent discussion of both qualitative and quantitative methods in adult education. Advantages, disadvantages, and cautions for some of the most common NIA methods are listed in Figure 3.2.

Regardless of the method or methods chosen for gathering data from the target population for the program offerings, one piece of information is essential to ensure that you have the best possible basis for plan-

TYPES OF NEEDS ASSESSMENT	ADVANTAGES	DISADVANTAGES	CAUTIONS	POSSIBLE POPULATIONS
Questionnaires	Relatively easy to develop Cost-effective Can be used with large numbers	No opportunity for clarification or follow-up	Pretest for reliability, validity, clarity	Current or potential program participants, community-wide sample or key consultants
Interview	Face-to-face interaction allows for clarification and follow-up Richness of detail even if group used	Lack of anonymity may affect responses Relatively expensive per person reached	Can be more subjectively interpreted Use a set question format to facilitate analysis	Current or potential program participants, community-wide sample or key consultants
Observation	Often more accurate than self-reported data for performance assessment Based on real rather than hypothetical situation	Time-consuming and expensive	Observers must be trained and checklist developed	Potential participants or individuals doing what participants will need to do
Standardized Tests	Developed by experts Checked for reliability and validity Can be used with large numbers	May not correlate well with performance May produce test anxiety	Don't overtest, especially early in a program Be sure to use tests appropriate for your population and purpose	Potential participants
Group Processes	Can be structured or unstructured Opportunity for clarification and follow-up	May be dominated by one or more members Possibility of "group think"	Facilitators must be trained Findings are subjective	Current and/or potential program participants or general public
Review of Records	Data is usually easy to access Solid data is collected rather than opinions or projections	May require permission Timelines may be a problem	Precautions must be taken to protect privacy	Current and/or potential program participants or general public

Figure 3.2 Six common methods of need and interest assessment

ning. It is not enough to know the topics your potential clients might be interested in. In addition to determining needs and interests, a good assessment procedure also addresses *intent to participate.* A person may be quite interested in landscape design and may need to learn to design databases on a computer, but the pressures of a job or the fact that mother, who recently had a heart attack, is moving in may severely limit participation in optional activities in the near future. The administrator who includes an opportunity for the potential learner to indicate intent to participate as well as need and interest receives much more accurate data on which to base programming decisions. The NIA also provides a perfect opportunity to gather input on preferred days, times, locations, and formats.

Determine Methods of Data Processing and Analysis. Will the data be gathered on machine-scannable sheets, or will it have to be entered by hand? How will the data be processed? Which analyses are most appropriate? Will the services of a programmer or data analyst be required? If all of these questions are not answered before the data collection begins, much time and effort can be wasted. It is essential that the individual who will asume responsibility for the data analysis be involved in the planning from the outset to ensure that the most economical and effective procedures are employed.

Develop a Timeline. One of the most valuable techniques to facilitate the completion of any group task is the development of a timeline which identifies when each component will be completed and who is responsible for each part. It is developed cooperatively among the responsible parties and each person or group involved receives a copy. Posting the timeline in a prominent place provides a constant reminder of the agreement and helps to ensure that all parties accomplish the tasks they accepted. A sample timeline is provided in Figure 3.3.

Conduct the NIA and Analyze the Data. As the NIA is conducted, the data is analyzed and the results reported, it becomes the job of the administrator to address any barriers to successful completion. Do workloads need to be adjusted due to unusual pressures on those who agreed to complete certain parts of the NIA? Has the computer center or print shop become backlogged, delaying the data analysis or production of the final report? Must timelines be adjusted, or can alternate arrangements be made?

Task	Responsible party	To be completed by
survey design (including methods of analysis)	T. Roberts & design team	January 15
survey review	Advisory committee	January 20
assembly of mailout materials	F. Jann & staff	January 22
contacts for other distribution	S. Hanover	January 22
survey distribution	Jann, Hanover & staff	January 25
data entry and analysis	J. Simkins	March 15
report preparation	T. Roberts	March 30

Figure 3.3 Sample timeline for design, implementation, and analysis of a survey as a part of NIA

Report the Results. The format and language of the report are determined by the audience, and there are often multiple audiences for NIA data in adult, community, and continuing education: advisory committees, parent organizations and/or boards of directors or trustees, the community at large, the media, and funding agencies, to name a few. Many adult education agencies or units find themselves preparing formal written reports accompanied by graphs and charts as well as less formal pieces such as fact sheets and news releases. Often overhead transparencies or informative charts or graphs are prepared to highlight major findings for oral presentations. Creating the visuals to emphasize your major points has become much easier. With the simplification of computer graphics packages, even virtual computer illiterates can create impressive graphs and charts.

Once these steps are completed, you should have an excellent idea of the needs and interests of your target population and the means to present this information effectively. Many of the same techniques can be incorporated into the other two major components of your NIA: gathering data from the community as a whole and examining the institutional experience base.

Gathering Data from the Community or Unit as a Whole

While input from individuals who are current or potential members of your target population is invaluable, it is also important to ensure that you have a broad perspective of the needs and interests of the community or service area as a whole. Converse with community leaders (especially those on your advisory committee), scan local media, attend or form interagency councils and make use of existing demographic data to develop an accurate overall view of the community and to ensure that your information remains current. Boone (1992) recommends collaboration with community leaders to study seven different dimensions of a community: population, institutional structure, social stratification, value system, informal social relationships, power structure, and ecology (divisions of the community in terms of social and economic functions, transportation, and housing areas and patterns).

Census data, now available on CD ROM, can be used alone or in combination with a geographic mapping program to pinpoint areas of need for certain types of programs, such as adult basic education, adult high school, or English as a second language. The data can be displayed on area maps by county, school district, neighborhood, or even at the block level (Andler, 1994; P. J. Guglielmino, personal communication, September 1992). A similar program can be used in combination with your enrollment data to display the segments of your target population that you are actually serving. Obviously, this process is maximally helpful in the years most closely following the collection of the census data; but do not discount the use of census data if the decade is drawing to a close. Often sample surveys or area surveys are done between the major collection efforts. Municipalities, counties, and states often conduct their own surveys. Contact your local chamber of commerce, city or county government, interagency council, or state department of labor or education to determine what is available and gain access. Your local librarian will probably be able to alert you to other useful resources, such as the closest university center for the study of population and special reports which may have been prepared by other agencies.

Examining the Institutional Experience Base

According to Nowlen (1980), "In practice, the most widespread needs assessment procedure in adult education consists of offering educational opportunities and then noting how many and what types of adults enroll" (p. 31). If your own institutional experience base, otherwise known as "what has worked in the past," is the only determiner of program content, the result is a static, unresponsive program that declines over time. While total reliance on past success as a predictor of future success is certainly unhealthy, it is unrealistic to downplay the role of current and past experience in the determination of program content.

Are there courses that have been continuously successful over time? Are there others that only "make" every third or fourth term? Are there logical follow-ups to courses now being offered? In addition to the more obvious, such as Spanish II or Accounting II, is the genealogy class interested in continuing to meet with a learning facilitator or resource person as they search for their own roots? Would the "Dealing with Divorce" participants like to form a support group and continue to meet with a facilitator (fee-producing) or on their own (community service)? Other aspects of your institutional experience base that might be sources of useful information include the results of previous needs and interests studies, accreditation self-studies, records of complaints or requests, and completion rates (Witkin, 1984).

While much can be gained from an examination of your own experience base, the successes and failures of similar programs are another valuable resource for planning. Networking at local, state, and national levels can help to identify hot topics and trends along with the hows and whys of offering them successfully; the horror stories of overly expensive or otherwise unsuccessful offerings are equally useful. Professional journals and local and national news media are other resources that can assist you in making sure that your program benefits from the experience of others. It is important to remember, however, that both the successes and failures of other programs are only an indicator. Whether these offerings would be viable in your program has to be decided on the basis of the understanding of your community that you and the advisory committee have developed.

Prioritize Needs and Interests

We have now discussed three major sources of information for determining program content that are included in the need and interest assessment (NIA): data gathered from individual learners who are a part of the target population, data from the community as a whole, and data reflecting the institutional experience base. Once you have collected this information or updated previous collection efforts, you will have an excellent base from which to begin the process of prioritizing individual, organizational, and community needs and interests that may be addressed by your program. As you do, a number of other considerations will emerge, and you will begin to screen the data you have collected through some qualitative and quantitative filters. Among them are your current institutional goals; projections of future needs within the community or organization, available in-house resources, such as personnel, time, money, space, and equipment; local, state, or federal guidelines or program standards; mandates of regulatory bodies; and the availability of other programs in the community which may address the needs and interests identified.

Develop Program Objectives

When you have considered the needs and interests in relation to these factors and prioritized them, you will be ready to translate them into program objectives. The literature reflects a great deal of controversy about this step in program planning. Szczypkowski (1980) comments, "There is no more crucial aspect of the program development process than objective setting, and no aspect is more misunderstood and misapplied" (p. 45). Sork and Caffarella (1989) report on disagreements relating to scope and level of specificity with which objectives should be stated. Both Boone (1992) and Szczypkowski (1980) attempt to address this concern, the latter with a pyramid-shaped objective-setting schema based on degree of specificity and expected time frame for achievement. Apps (1985) points out that it may be impossible to anticipate all of the necessary or appropriate objectives of a program at the outset and warns of the danger of limiting program flexibility and responsiveness because of a need to meet preset objectives. Apps (1985) and Brookfield (1986) question whether objectives should be stated in behavioral form, a practice which has been widely debated but largely accepted since Mager (1962) advocated it. Jones (1982) questions whether objectives should be stated at all.

Certainly legitimate differences of opinion and variations in means of arriving at and stating objectives exist. Despite the controversy surrounding this topic, the vast majority of writers on program development recommend that objectives be used. The development of objectives is an extremely valuable part of the program planning process. The need to set objectives provides a forum for deciding on major program thrusts and levels of expected achievement; the objectives themselves provide guidelines for action and a basis for program evaluation. Whether or not the objectives are optimally stated is a secondary consideration.

Most of the confusion about objectives related to scope and specificity appears to be attributable to two factors: multiple meanings of the term *program*, and failure to differentiate between *program objectives* (the macro view) and *learning objectives* for a specific course or activity (the micro view). The word *program* is routinely used to refer to all of the offerings of an educational unit, as in the continuing education program at the University. Just as routinely, it is used to refer to a specific grouping of courses or activites within that program, often based on topic (Legal Assistants' Program, Great Books Program) or target audience (Senior Learners' Program, Business and Industry Services). These are the macro levels—the levels at which program objectives are appropriate. In any program, there may be further subdivisions until the level of learning objectives for a specific course or activity is reached. Although behavioral objectives (stated in terms of measurable behavior the learners will exhibit) are generally recommended (Boone, 1992; Boyle & Jahns, 1970; Cranton, 1989; Sork & Caffarella, 1989), it is often awkward or infeasible to state comprehensive program objectives in measurable, behavioral terms, especially those related to the affective domain. In actuality, Mager (1962,1975), in his two books which are most often cited in discussions of behavioral objectives, was recommending their use at the course or instructional level (learning objectives), not the program level. The danger in overemphasis on behaviorally stated objectives is that administrators and program planners may become frustrated in their efforts to devise logical ways to state affective objectives in a behavioral format and decide to omit them entirely. When this occurs, the learners will ultimately suffer. Programs are evaluated on the basis of their objectives, and if affective objectives are not included, learning facilitators may be led to focus only on what is observable and quantifiable. One cannot easily quantify or always observe the development of a love of learning, a commitment to lifelong learning, a more positive self-concept, or a greater acceptance of new ideas or cultures other than one's own; yet these may be some of the most important things to be learned in adult, community, and continuing education settings. It is at the course or activity level (learning objective level) that the use of behavioral objectives becomes maximally beneficial, but cautions still need to be observed. This topic will be discussed further in the next section, at the learning objective level.

The concern about prestated objectives limiting flexibility and program responsiveness raised by Apps (1985) can be addressed by setting up a periodic review of progress, with the understanding that it will include not only an examination of progress toward the achievement of initially stated objectives but will also determine if objectives should be altered or added to in order to best serve the needs of the learners.

Design Educational Offerings

The heart of an educational program serving individual adults and the community in which they live is the course or activity level. Regardless of how lofty the institutional mission or supporting goals might be, the program will be dysfunctional if the vision and care used in developing those goals is not reflected in the classes, seminars, workshops, community forums, and other activities which are the point of contact for the learner and the learning facilitator. The design of specific educational opportunities is, in many ways, a microcosm of the program design process: it involves its own needs and interest assessment, the setting of objectives, development of strategies, implementation, and evaluation.

Although a detailed discussion of this process is beyond the scope of this chapter, a few major points will be highlighted. It is the role of the adult, community, or continuing education adminstrator, as instructional leader, to ensure that all of the individuals involved in designing activities at this level are fully aware of the goals and purposes of the educational institution or unit and are also capable of creating effective learning environments. They should be aware of the characteristics of adult learners and familiar with a wide range of learning formats, activities, and resources. Following the practice at the macro level, they should be encouraged to seek learner input in the design process. There are many good references for those unfamiliar with ways of involving learners in program design, such as Caffarella (1994), Cervero and Wilson (1994), Dean (1994), and Knowles (1980).

In terms of learning objectives, it is at this level that the phrasing of desired outcomes in behavioral terms has several distinct advantages. A behavioral objective is stated in terms of the learner, and includes:

1. Performance (what the learner is to be able to do)

2. Conditions (important conditions under which the performance is expected to occur)

3. Criterion (the quality or level of performance that will be considered acceptable) (Mager, 1975, p. 23).

The most important benefit of the use of this format is the change of focus from teacher or facilitator behavior to learner behavior. It becomes clear that it is not what is taught or offered that is central, but what the participants actually learn. The incorporation of some specific measure of success is also a plus, encouraging learning facilitators to set specific goals and providing a benchmark for evaluation. One can readily see that this type of objective format is extremely useful for stating objectives in the cognitive or psychomotor domains, as the following examples illustrate.

ABE class-cognitive objective
Upon completion of 60 hours of instruction (condition), the participants' reading comprehension scores will increase (learner performance) by an average of one grade level (criterion).

Golf class-psychomotor objective
After 20 hours of instruction (condition), participants' golf scores will decrease (learner performance) by an average of 5 points (criterion).

Objectives such as these are easily developed and stated and provide clear and understandable goals; however, a problem often occurs when one attempts to state affective objectives in this form. One can identify suitable measurements for some affective areas, such as attitude toward reading, because a number of valid and reliable assessments are readily available. But how does one reliably measure increased confidence in one's golf game or interest in the sport? Obviously, these would be expected outcomes of a golf class, and it is certainly possible to devise measures for them, but the reliability and feasibility of the measures would be dubious and the incidence of testing could become onerous. This difficulty with stating affective outcomes in measureable form can lead frustrated program designers to leave out the desired affective outcomes—an unfortunate consequence, since they are often as important as or more important than the cognitive or psychomotor outcomes. The effective adult, community, and continuing education administrator must ensure that form follows function and not the reverse: the needs and interests of the adult learners are paramount, and affective objectives cannot be ignored simply because they are difficult to state in measureable form.

Implement and Evaluate Programs

The implementation and evaluation of programs, the last two steps in the program development model, are addressed in other chapters of this book. The chapters which relate to the implementation process include Chapter 4, Budgeting and Financing; Chapter 5, Selecting and Developing Staff; Chapter 6, Marketing and Public Relations; and Chapter 8, Legal and Ethical Considerations. Evaluation is discussed in Chapter

7. Please note that evaluation results from previous offerings constitute an important input for the NIA for future offerings.

SUMMARY

The determination of content for programs serving adult learners must go beyond the traditional discrepancy-focused needs assessment approach. This chapter presents a more comprehensive approach based on a new program development model. At the macro, or comprehensive program level, the process begins with a review of unit or institutional purpose. Needs and interest assessment (NIA) data are then drawn from three major sources: the current and potential target population, the community as a whole, and the institutional experience base. Identified needs and interests are then prioritized in light of a number of internal and external factors, such as current goals, available resources, availability of other programs which can address or are addressing some of the identified needs and interests, possible cooperative efforts, and projections of future needs. Once the needs and interests are prioritized, programming goals and objectives are developed, completing the determination of program content at the macro or comprehensive program level. Determination of program content at the course or activity level then proceeds, as each educational activity is designed in what can be viewed as a microcosm of the larger process. During this phase, the role of the adult, community, or continuing education administrator shifts; rather than being actively involved in the process, the administrator serves primarily as an interpreter of program purpose and goals, a resource person or resource procurer, and a supervisor or performance evaluator. Program evaluation is continual throughout both the micro and macro phases, with input from learners, advisory board members, faculty, and staff serving as important triggers for adaptation and revision throughout the process as well as at specified intervals, such as the end of an individual course or activity (micro) or the end of a fiscal year or program year (macro).

CHAPTER 4

Budgeting and Financing

Employing sound financial management is an important goal in adult, community, and continuing education. Because so many programs run on a break-even or profit basis, administrators are subject to some form of financial management and budget constraints. Nearly every organization in adult, community, and continuing education must show some degree of accountability to its constituencies, and this is often accomplished, at least in part, through the budget. Matkin (1985) suggests that several recent trends have lead many administrators in adult, community, and continuing education to place greater emphasis on the budget process and to learn more about the theories behind budgeting and financial control. He identifies these as sharply decreasing funding for higher education, increasing emphasis on multiple source funding, and greater reliance on self-support budgeting. Shipp (1982) contends that "the tools for sound financial management are at hand . . . and concepts such as market research, target populations, segmentation of population, promotion, advertising, and accounting have entered the lexicon of effective continuing education administrators" (pp. 5–6). This chapter focuses on some of the tools for sound financial planning and management. We begin with a definition of budgeting and its purposes. Next, several types of budgets are described and some key terms defined. A sample budget follows along with some discussion about how to augment funding through the identification of income sources such as grants or external awards.

DEFINITION AND PURPOSES OF BUDGETS

There is a fair amount of literature dealing with budgeting in adult, community, and continuing education and some consistency in defining the term. For example, Matkin (1985) defines *budgeting* as "a process of planning the future operations of an organization and systematically comparing those plans with actual results" (p. 5). Similarly, Holmberg-Wright (1982) sees budgeting as "a written document of what an individual or organization expects to do in the future expressed in quantitative or monetary terms" (p. 24). Kowalski (1988) views the budget as "a document outlining a plan of financial operations. Specifically, it sets forth an estimate of proposed expenditures for a given period or purpose and the proposed means of financing those expenditures" (p. 162). Strother and Klus (1982) also emphasize the translation of intended activities into quantitative terms, but stress that "budgeting must be a continuing activity, not something that is done annually or biennially" (p. 207).

Budgets can serve a number of important purposes for any organization. Most of these purposes occur simultaneously, are related and overlapping, and may at times conflict. Matkin (1985) believes that budgets often embody goals of an organization, may be used to develop standards of performance, can motivate employees to perform at high levels, and also serve as a means of improving communication at all organizational levels. Similarly, Strother and Klus (1982) see the budget as a document that helps improve the organization. They view this document serving five important purposes:

1. *Planning.* As a statement of intended activities it is the outcome of a close look at problems and opportunities and an evaluation of alternative ways of dealing with them; it involves forecasting future developments and shaping the future by the actions we take.

2. *Delegation.* By setting goals and allocating resources for their accomplishment, higher levels of administration can assign authority for execution of elements of the overall plan to lower levels of the organization, with less need for close monitoring than would be necessary if the plan existed only in the minds of higher level administrators.

3. *Coordination.* Since the plan describes a set of interrelated activities, it frees the various participants to carry out their part of the plan without excessive checking with those responsible for other parts of the plan; like a good set of blueprints, it enables the various specialized functions to be carried out without having to change plans or improvise because the plumbers, electricians, and heating engineers all want to run their conduits between the same two studs.

4. *Control.* Because of human error and unforeseen events the best laid plans can go wrong; the budget sets financial standards of perform-

ance so that deviations from the plan can be detected and timely corrective action taken.

5. *Performance review.* As a record of intentions the budget provides a basis for evaluating the degree to which the intended activities were successfully carried out; it helps identify the strong and weak spots in a plan, providing a foundation for future improvements, and the elimination of sources of trouble.

TYPES OF BUDGETS

There are many different types of budgets in use today. Depending on the size and complexity of the adult, community, continuing education organization, budgets may be prepared at the programming level on up through the entire organization. Thus, financial planning often takes the form of a hierarchy, with *course budgets* usually prepared by program planners at the lowest level and *master budgets* usually prepared by top-level administrators to reflect the entire financial picture of the organization. Preparing both types of budgets are essential in adult, community, and continuing education since they help plan for the future and avoid unpleasant surprises that could lead to financial ruin. The more that budgets are linked to program planning, implementation, and evaluation, the greater the odds of success.

Format Types

Budgets are often classified by formats. Two of the most common are *program budget* and *line item budget*. A program budget typically includes any sponsored activity by the adult, community, continuing education organization that lists the projected income and expenses of a particular endeavor. A line item budget identifies the income and expenses of the organization without reference to the program or its associated purpose. For example, a line item budget might list all publicity costs on one line, whereas a program budget would divide the publicity costs among the number of participants. Line item budgets are very common in organizational budgeting but are less helpful to program planners (Matkin, 1985).

Budgets may also be classified according to their intended purpose.

Operating budgets cover the broadest range and show the revenues, expenses, and related items for a given period of time such as a fiscal year. *Capital budgets* cover the acquisition of equipment, facilities, and other assets that are expected to return value to the organization over an extended period of time. For example, acquiring a new building or enlarging existing classroom facilities would be items in a capital budget. *Cash budgets* show the anticipated sources and uses of cash in an organization. They are intended to make sure that the organization does not run out of money so that expenses are met and excess revenue is invested wisely.

Cash budgets may also be linked to two other types of budgets: *financial budgets* and *expenditure budgets*. Financial budgets are concerned with the sources of funding for an organization. Income from tuition, program fees, or donor awards are examples of funding sources. Expenditure budgets concentrate less on the sources of income and more on on where and how resources will be spent. Most organizations in adult, community, and continuing education use expenditure budgeting although it is becoming increasingly important to pay attention to sources of funds (Matkin, 1985).

Other Types

Budgets may also be categorized according to whether they are *fixed* or *variable*. In practical terms, both types of budgets are used frequently in adult, community, and continuing education and depend on the types of anticipated income and expenses. A fixed budget assumes a certain volume of business will occur over a specified time period and appropriate dollar amounts are allocated for each category of expense. Comparisons can then be made based on actual costs and budgeted costs.

A variable budget is based on a range of volume or activity and is widely used at the program planning level. Some examples of variable costs include handouts, textbooks, food, and other consumable items. Registration fees and tuition dollars are examples of variable income sources. Both estimates of variable costs and income interact with each other since one is dependent on the other. However, there are also fixed expenses such as marketing, instructor salaries, and facility rentals that are independent of the number of enrollments. These are usually referred to as *sunk costs* that will be either lost or absorbed by the parent institution regardless of whether the event is offered.

Variable budgets can be very useful in successful program planning in adult, community, and continuing education since three classes of costs are recognized. First, variable costs associated with the purchase of materials or consumables can be identified. For instance, if a textbook or software program is required of each participant, the total cost of the materials increases in relation to the number enrolled.

Second, semivariable costs may be calculated depending on the volume of activity generated. For example, janitorial services may not change significantly with a slight increase in enrollments. But if the number of weekend courses doubled, then additional expenses would be required for expanded janitorial services.

Third, fixed costs such as depreciation of equipment, administrative expense, or building rental may remain the same regardless of fluctuating enrollments. However, as enrollments increase and income rises, fixed costs should fall due to the expanding activity. This scenario is ideal, especially in adult, community, and continuing education (Holmberg-Wright, 1982).

BUDGET APPROACHES

There are many different approaches to budgeting and they all share the common goal of improving organizational performance through sound financial management. Although there are a number of different acronyms in the literature describing various budget approaches, most can be categorized according to *traditional budgeting* and *program budgeting*. Knowing something about these approaches is useful in developing a deeper understanding of the budgetary process and strengthening our administrative competence.

Traditional Budgeting

Traditional budgeting has been used for many years in all kinds of public and private institutions with a good deal of success. In the early years, traditional budgeting was synonymous with line item budgeting where a listing of income and expenditure categories were assigned to a line on a page. Budgeting under this method literally meant control of the line items.

In more recent years, line item budgeting has given way to its more contemporary brethren, incremental budgeting. Under this method, each budgetary line item is evaluated for an incremental adjustment or remains unadjusted in the base (Holmberg-Wright, 1982). According to Matkin (1985), "Incremental budgeting has the advantage of focusing management's attention on the important changes occurring in an organization. It also involves relatively little computational time and effort, since the bulk of the budget, represented by the base, is automatically defined and easily calculated. However, incremental budgeting has the drawback of suppressing the review of established programs, which might, by virtue of being hidden in the base, continue to be funded long after they are useful" (p. 11). To correct for such problems, Matkin notes that zero-based budgeting (ZBB) came into vogue in the private sector but this method has largely been a failure because of the time and effort required to justify the value of every program and the entire budget annually.

Program Budgeting

Because of the nature and mission of most organizations in adult, community, and continuing education, program budgeting has become the preferred approach to sound financial management and has a number of advantages of over traditional budgeting. Chief among these is a closer relationship between the desired ends in an organization and the means through which they are accomplished. Holmberg-Wright (1982) believes that program budgeting helps organizations achieve better coordination between planning and budgeting, promotes analysis of various consequences of budgeting decisions, improves an understanding of how proposed expenditures influence programs, and allows the budget to facilitate greater congruence between an organization's goals and its programs. Strother and Klus (1982) contend that program budgeting is useful in adult, community, and continuing education since it helps answer the following questions:

1. What do we want to do?

2. Why do we want to do it?

3. How will we do it?

4. What do we need in order to do it?

5. How will we know whether we have succeeded?

Clearly, most organizations in adult, community, and continuing education, if they have not already, will want to adopt program budgeting as the primary tool for managing various human and financial resources. Matkin (1985) notes that this is fairly easy to do since the nature of adult, community, and continuing education is to produce programs of some kind. Holmberg-Wright (1982) agrees, but stresses the importance of using program budgeting throughout the organization.

DEVELOPING A SUCCESSFUL BUDGET: SOME USEFUL TIPS

Successful planning and budgeting in adult, community, and continuing education is dependent on the execution of a number of procedures so that accurate information is obtained on which to prepare a budget. As noted earlier, a budget is a planning tool that identifies anticipated revenue and costs that supports the mission of the adult, community, and continuing education organization. It is overly simplistic to argue that there is one set of procedures for all types of budgeting. At the same time, Holmberg-Wright (1982) identifies four budgetary procedures, or phases that work especially well in adult, community, and continuing education because they combine planning with the budgetary process. The four phases are (1) establishing financial goals, (2) formulating plans, (3) preparing the budget document, and (4) evaluating the budget and the sponsoring adult, community, and continuing education organization. Each phase is described briefly to help you formulate an overall planning and budget strategy that can be employed in your own adult, community, and continuing education setting.

Financial Goals

The first phase in building a successful budget is for administrators to set financial goals for the organization that are based on projected revenue and anticipated costs over a specific period of time. This time period is usually referred to as the *fiscal year*, and helps relate short-term planning objectives to long-term budgetary goals for the organization. Forecasting techniques are often employed at this point as well as evaluation results from previously sponsored programs so that risks are minimized and appropriate financial goals established. Once the financial goals are established, administrators communicate them to various program planners within the organization for implementation of the next phase.

Plans

The second phase involves formulating plans that show anticipated revenue and expenses for the various programs to be offered. Each program planner is asked to calculate the cost of offering the courses, anticipated enrollments, course fees and associated expenses, and the expected revenue to be realized from the educational offerings. The administration then assembles all of these individual budgets into a total budget for the organization.

Document Preparation

The third phase involves the actual preparation of the budget document by the administration. The total budget is computed based on submissions by the various program planners and their respective units such as conferencing, noncredit services, academic credit programs, advising and counseling services, telecommunications and independent studies, etc. Budgets are generally organized according to income and disbursements expressed as *budget statements*. Each budget statement lists estimated income and all costs of programing including direct expenses for operating the program and indirect expenses that are charged for providing the necessary services to offer the program.

A key element in preparing the actual budget document is effective communication among all parties involved. Both administration and program planners should be working together to understand the budget process, expected target levels to gauge performance, and what decisions are necessary to ensure programmatic success throughout the organization.

Records and Evaluation

The fourth and final phase involves keeping good financial records so that the budgetary process and programming activities sponsored by the adult, community, and continuing education organization can be evaluated. Administrators and program planners can use the budget document to evaluate progress and the extent to which goals for the organizations are being met. Developing and using monthly financial reports and accompanying program planning records helps all members of the organization see the results of their hard work and ensures a higher level of accountability (Holmberg-Wright, 1982).

SUCCESSFUL PROGRAM BUDGETING: AN ILLUSTRATED EXAMPLE

In our discussion so far, we have looked at how budgeting is defined, reviewed some approaches to budgeting, and presented a four-phase process for developing a budget. This preliminary information is useful in understanding some of the basics of budgeting and how it relates to successful programming in adult, community, and continuing education. We now turn to an application of this information by illustrating a sample budget.

Figure 4.1 shows a budget form that might be used at the program planning level in an adult, community, and continuing education organization; one we will use in our example below. Note that the form contains some basic information about the program, who is responsible for the program, and a space for administrative approval. Also note that the form is organized according to three major categories: income, direct expenses, and indirect expenses. Remember that *income* is usually figured according to the number of fee-paying participants, *direct* expenses refer to such items as travel, mailings, handouts, lodging, instructor fees, and so forth, and *indirect expenses* refer to administrative costs provided by the sponsoring agency usually figured on a participant basis such as $7.50 per person or a percentage of the direct expenses. At the bottom of the form is a box designed to calculate the number of participants needed to break even, meet program expenses, and carry the program. These calculations are essential since they help the program planner make informed decisions about the status of a program. For example, there are occasions when it is prudent to offer a program that meets basic expenses but does not contribute any income to the organization. Such a program could be a pilot effort designed to build long-term interest in a subject area and, therefore, substantial profits in the future.

Program No. _____ Dates _____
Program Name _____
Program Specialist _____ Director Budget _____ Date _____
Credit Hours _____ Approved Final Report _____ Date _____
Noncredit Hours _____

INCOME		BUDGETED				ACTUAL	SUNK
		Variable		Fixed	Total	Total Participants	
	A	Per Person	Total				
1. Registrants # _____ @ $ _____							
2. _____							
TOTAL							

DIRECT EXPENSES

1. a. Honorariums _____							
_____							
_____							
b. Aides _____							
c. Payroll Taxes _____							
2. Contract Services _____							
3. Telephone _____							
4. Travel: Office _____							
Instructor/Participant_____							
5. Handouts _____							
6. Mailing _____							
7. Advertising & Promotion _____							
a. Brochures #_____ $_____							
b. Flyers # _____ $_____							
c. Postage # _____ $_____							
8. Lodging _____							
9. Equipment Rentals _____							
10. Facility Rentals _____							
11. Food Services _____							
_____							
_____							
12. Program Supplies & Other Exp. _____							
_____							
_____							
13. Secretarial Services _____							
14. Contingency _____							
Subtotal	B			C			

INDIRECT EXPENSES

	$	Administrative Fees	D		E

	TOTAL	
	Net Income	

Number of Participants Necessary to:

A. Break Even $= \dfrac{C + D}{A - B} =$ _____ = _____

B. Meet Program Expenses $= \dfrac{C}{A - B} =$ _____ = _____

C. Carry the Program $= \dfrac{C - E}{A - B} =$ _____ = _____

Figure 4.1 Program budget sheet

TRAINING PROGRAM FOR
APPRENTICESHIP INSTRUCTORS

The program we will use to illustrate the budget process is a training program for apprenticeship instructors. Sarah, a program planning specialist, works for a community college located in an urban area of approximately 600,000 people. She has conducted numerous needs assessments, met with key informants and organizational leaders, and on the basis of this information, believes a special program is needed for instructors of apprentice electricians. The instructors are highly skilled craftsmen, who work during the day in supervisory capacities but have little or no formal training in teaching, curriculum development, and classroom assessment. Sarah believes that a program organized over four consecutive days with the option of carrying academic credit is ideal. She has worked with the vocational education department at the community college and the faculty are interested in delivering the program but need help in determining whether it is a cost-effective venture. Sarah assures them that it is and demonstrates her contention through a budget she developed. Follow along as she explains the budget process and some assumptions she is working with.

Sarah begins by emphasizing that a well-designed budget should provide three essential financial items: (1) The number of participants needed to breakeven, (2) The extent of risk, and (3) The point at which the cost to cancel is equal to the cost to operate. She says that there are a number of facts available to prepare the program budget and that the program costs as well as indirect costs (administrative fees) must be covered to operate the program. In the case of the instructor training program, she assumes the following:

1. Meal charges are $25 per day per participant (or $100 total) and lodging is $120 for the four days.

2. Four instructors are to be paid $800 each (or $3,200 total). If the program is canceled, each instructor will need $100 to cover expenses.

3. Advertising will cost $400 for an ad in a regional trade magazine and $425 for a direct-mail brochure. Postage will cost $300.

4. Telephone costs will be $50.

5. Equipment rentals for overheads, video machines, and computers will be $200. Facility rentals for use of an auditorium, several classrooms, and breakout rooms will be $250.

6. Awards and prizes for selected participants will cost $125.

7. Other per person expenses include:
   a. A 3-ring binder for each participant ($4).
   b. Curriculum material for each participant ($8).
   c. Morning and afternoon breaks for 4 days (total - $10).
   d. Paper and pencils, etc. ($2).
   e. Closing banquet ($10).

8. A total of 200 participants are expected to enroll at a per person fee of $350 for a total income of $70,000.

Sarah shows the faculty the actual budget based on the above figures (see Figure 4.2). She explains how each line is calculated according to the expected income, direct expenses, and indirect expenses. She also notes the importance of calculating a contingency fee so that sunk costs can be recovered in the event something catastrophic occurs or the program fails to make. By her calculations, the program stands to turn a healthy profit of just under $10,000 assuming the enrollment figures are met.

But Sarah does not stop there. She does some additional analysis to show the faculty how many participants are need to break even (96 participants), how many are needed to meet program expenses (81 participants), and how many are needed to carry the program (63 participants). By calculating these numbers, Sarah is assessing the extent of risk involved in offering the program and showing the faculty what they need to do to ensure success. Sarah may also use the figures to see if the faculty are comfortable with the program fee for participants or if they wish to reduce it to a less costly level.

By using a systematic approach to budgeting, Sarah has taken a substantial amount of the guesswork out of program planning. She has used a powerful tool to demonstrate to her clients and superiors that a successful program will likely occur unless unforeseen events happen. Indeed, the unexpected can happen, but usually with solid program planning and budget analysis, the risks are minimized considerably.

AUGMENTING THE FINANCIAL BASE

Most organizations in adult, community, and continuing education use creative ways of augmenting the financial base since sole reliance on

Program No. _O31_

Program Name _Training Program for Apprenticeship Instructors_

Program Specialist _Sarah_   Director Budget _D-O31_   Date _Today's Date_

Credit Hours _Optional_   Approved Final Report ____   Date _Today's Date_

Noncredit Hours _Optional_

INCOME	BUDGETED				ACTUAL	SUNK
	Variable		Fixed	Total	Total Participants	
	Per Person	Total				
A						
1. Registrants # _200_ @ $ _350_	350	70,000		70,000		
2. ____						
TOTAL						

DIRECT EXPENSES						
1. a. Honorariums _4 Faculty ($800 each)_			3,200	3,200		
___Expenses for 4 Faculty___						400
b. Aides ____						
c. Payroll Taxes ____						
2. Contract Services ____						
3. Telephone ____			50	50		50
4. Travel: Office ____						
Instructor/Participant____						
5. Handouts ____						
6. Mailing ____						
7. Advertising & Promotion ____			400	400		400
a. Brochures #____ $____			425	425		425
b. Flyers # ____ $____						
c. Postage # ____ $____			300	300		300
8. Lodging ____	120	24,000		24,000		
9. Equipment Rentals ____			200	200		
10. Facility Rentals ____			250	250		
11. Food Services _Meals_	100	20,000		20,000		
___A.M. & P.M. Breaks___	10	2,000		2,000		
___Banquet___	10	2,000		2,000		
12. Program Supplies & Other Exp. ____	4	800		800		
			125	125		125
	10	2,000		2,000		
13. Secretarial Services ____						
14. Contingency _5% of Direct Expenses_			2,785	2,785		
Subtotal	B 254	50,800	C 7,735	58,535		
$ 7.50 Administrative Fees				D 1,500		E 1,700

INDIRECT EXPENSES

	TOTAL	68,000	
	Net Income	9,965	

Number of Participants Necessary to:	A. Break Even = $\frac{C + D}{A - B}$ = $\frac{9,235}{96}$ = 96
	B. Meet Program Expenses = $\frac{C}{A - B}$ = $\frac{7,735}{96}$ = 81
	C. Carry the Program = $\frac{C - E}{A - B}$ = $\frac{6,035}{96}$ = 63

Figure 4.2 Program budget sheet—budget illustration

participant tuition or fees is risky. For example, income sources may come from organization subsidies, auxiliary enterprises and sales, grants and contracts, government funds, and profits from the educational unit itself. Caffarella (1994) provides the following brief description of these income sources along with examples:

1. *Organization subsidy.* The educational function receives operating funds from the parent organization.

    Example: The Office of Staff Development receives an expense budget of $150,000 annually for salaries, materials and equipment, travel, general office supplies, and printing.

2. *Participant fees.* Participants are charged a fee for attending a program.

    Example: Eighty percent of all adult education programs sponsored by the local school district must break even. Thus the participants' fees must cover all expenses of those programs.

3. *Auxiliary enterprises and sales.* Revenue is earned from the sale of materials, publications, and services provided by the educational unit to other organizations and individuals.

    Example: A nationally prominent accounting firm has developed an excellent computer-based training program and is now selling it to other organizations for profit.

4. *Grants and contracts from foundations and other private organizations.* Private foundations and other private organizations award funds to an educational unit to develop a specific program. Usually these awards go to nonprofit organizations.

    Example: An award is given to a nonprofit hospital to develop a specific program on the prevention of AIDS.

5. *Government funding (federal, state, and local).* Government funds are awarded or given to an educational unit to develop a specific program. These funds may be given to for-profit or nonprofit agencies (depending on the regulations governing the funds).

    Example: A local community college, in partnership with a private business, is awarded a grant to initiate a job training program from unemployed workers.

6. *Profit from the educational unit.* The educational unit produces an overall profit from the operation, which in turn can be used for future programs.

Example: The College of Continuing Education at XYZ University on average nets a 10 percent profit from the Conferences and Institutes Division, which is used to sponsor new program ventures.

Skilled program planners in adult, community, and continuing education are adept at broadening the financial base. They are always on the lookout for additional funding sources and often ask clients for leads and possible contacts. Sarah, in working with the vocational education faculty for the apprenticeship training program, found that her state department of education could provide funding assistance to selected participants if a grant were written. She worked with the faculty coordinator in writing the grant and ended up securing $50,000 for use in reducing the participants' registration fee. This was greatly appreciated by the program sponsors and because the program was a better value, significantly more people enrolled resulting in substantial profits. As Sarah later confided to her director, "we had many happy problems!"

Just as it is important to estimate the expenses associated with a program in preparing a budget, it is equally important to identify all possible income sources. Figure 4.3 may be used as a worksheet for estimating program income.

SUMMARY

This chapter focused on some of the tools for employing sound financial management in adult, community, and continuing education. It began with a definition of budgeting and its purposes. Next, several types of budgets were discussed and some key terms defined. A sample budget was presented with an accompanying illustration showing how an actual budget in adult, continuing, an community education might be prepared. Finally, the chapter closed with some discussion of how to augment the financial base through identifying various income sources. We now turn our attention to selecting and developing staff in adult, community, and continuing education.

Income Source	Amount of Income/Subsidy

1. Organizational subsidy (describe)

   _____

   _____

   _____ $_____

2. Participant fee (fee X number of estimated participants)

  _____ X _____ $_____
     Fee   # of participants

3. Auxiliary enterprises and sales (item or service to be sold X number of estimated customers)

  _____ X _____ $_____
   Item/Service   # of participants

4. Grants and contracts (list each source of funding with amount):

   A. _____ $_____

   B. _____ $_____

   C. _____ $_____

5. Government funds (list each source of funding with amount):

   A. _____ $_____

   B. _____ $_____

   C. _____ $_____

6. Profit from the educational unit $_____

                   Total Income $_____

Figure 4.3 Worksheet for estimating income sources. Adapted from Caffarella (1994).

CHAPTER 5

Selecting and Developing Staff

Adult, community, and continuing education organizations could not function successfully without competent, motivated, and well-trained staff; however, "a surprisingly neglected consideration is the amount and type of attention that is given to staff development" (Knox, 1991, p. 236). Strother and Klus (1982) suggest that staffing is a logical outgrowth of two of the basic functions of administration—planning and organizing. Staff are needed to perform four essential functions: administration, planning and implementing programs, teaching, and support (this could range from custodial services to coordinating or managing responsibilities). In a large-scale organization these functions may be performed by specialists, while in a small-scale operation one person may perform all of these functions. As Hall (1980) states, "Effective staffing is essential to any productive organization but it is not often accomplished well without a plan" (p. 181).

The purpose of this chapter is to present a staffing plan that articulates a process for identifying the roles and responsibilities of staff, an approach for selecting staff, and to introduce strategies for communicating job expectations and for developing staff. Powers (1992) writes that staff "will perform with excellence if they have well-defined jobs, are capable of doing the job, know what is expected of them, have the tools to do the job, have the necessary skills and knowledge, receive feedback on how well they perform, and perceive and receive rewards for performing as desired" (p. 8). While the word *staff* can mean a paid or voluntary position such as instructor, tutor, support personnel, planner, coordinator, or administrator, this chapter for illustrative purposes will focus on the instructor role. Many times the strategies for paid versus volunteer staffing are presented as unique and separate entities. The plan presented in this chapter suggests that the same strategies should be utilized for all paid and voluntary staffing regardless of the position.

DEFINING JOB ROLES
AND RESPONSIBILITIES

Before the staff selection process begins, a job definition or description must be developed. The job description reflects what the job's function is and why the position exists. Job specifications or requirements reflect the knowledge, skills, experiences, qualifications, and characteristics deemed necessary for the individual to successfully carry out the responsibilities of the position.

Defining the Job

A good job description as mentioned above reflects the job's functions and why the position exists. The description developed should stem from the mission or goals of the organization. If the purpose of the organization is to provide adult basic education (ABE) programs in a particular geographic area, then as a paid or voluntary instructor in the ABE program your purpose is to provide educational activities that enable adult learners in the program to perform more effectively, for example, in reading and writing at a particular level. To accomplish this, the instructor is responsible for not only engaging in instruction but for the preparational aspects of instruction and for the evaluation of the results of the instruction. Each of the three areas can have numerous responsibilities connected to them. Therefore, a well-developed job description will point out the areas of responsibility of the instructor.

Requirements of the Job

In addition, a good job description will identify the knowledge, skills, experiences, qualifications, and characteristics required for the job. Let's look briefly at each of the required areas and some of the elements connected to each. Drawing heavily from the scheme Powers (1992) has developed for the training and development sector, we suggest his process works very effectively in adult, community, and continuing education settings as well. For our purpose, the constructed job description will be for instructors in a noncredit continuing education program that offers simple to complex course offerings.

Knowledge

What is knowledge? What should be the level of knowledge required of instructors within the organization? The term *knowledge* refers to the state of knowing about or understanding something. The level of knowledge required by the instructor depends upon the course. The following list identifies and defines the areas of knowledge, regardless of level, required of instructors in our noncredit continuing education program:

- knowledge of how adults learn
- knowledge of adults participating in program
- knowledge of subject matter
- knowledge of the organizations involved
- knowledge required for specific job

Skills

What do we mean by the term *skill?* Skills are abilities in which an instructor is proficient or capable of being proficient. The level of skill required by the instructor will depend upon the nature and complexity of the course. Listed below are some basic skills required of the instructor within the classroom:

- climate-setting skills
- verbal skills
- interpersonal skills
- leadership skills
- platform skills
- decision-making skills
- flexibility
- analytical skills
- problem-solving skills
- risk-taking skills
- ability to manage diverse groups
- relevant skills

Experience

The term *experience* refers to those things an individual has done or events he or she has lived through. For example, an instructor of a computer course is most likely to possess some hands-on computer experience. If the course is technical in nature, the instructor will be expected to have some technical experience. The nature of the course will depend upon what type and kind of experience is most desirable for the instructor. Typically, it is desired that instructors possess some or all of the following experiences:

- skills experience
- technical experience
- teaching experience
- other experiences

Qualifications

Qualifications refer to those conditions that must be met to do something. To instruct in some courses, a degree or license may be required while in other noncredit program offerings it is not. Again, the qualifications desired depends on the nature of the course and the expectations of the instructor. Basic qualifications required or desired of instructors may be:

- college degree
- license
- certificate
- train-the-trainer course
- significant instructional experiences
- other qualifications

Characteristics

The word *characteristics* refers to those traits that constitute a person's character. As Powers (1992) states, "the traits required of instructors depends of the nature of the course materials and the nature of the organization" (p. 19). He suggests that an effective way to identify the required characteristics of instructors is to examine the values of the organization itself. The following characteristics may be desired or required of the instructor:

- high level of energy
- enthusiasm
- strong sense of commitment
- integrity

- ability to model desired behaviors and skills
- self-directed
- ability to seek and accept feedback

Putting it into a Form

Now that we have identified the elements of defining job roles and responsibilities, we can transfer what we have under each heading above to the appropriate headings on the "Job Description and Requirements" form (see Figure 5.1). By having all this information on a form, it assists the agency or program administrator in understanding how the job supports the goals of the organization and the requirements of the job as well as makes visible the major and subordinate responsibilities of the job.

While we have illustrated the process for an instructor, this process can be easily adapted to other staffing positions, whether paid or voluntary in nature. By utilizing this process, it not only helps to identify the most salient elements of each particular job, but it also assists you as the agency or program administrator in justifying why certain positions exist and how they support the organizational goals and mission.

SELECTING STAFF

Now that you have defined the job and the allied skills and responsibilities associated with it, selecting the right candidate to fill the position is your next step. Selecting staff should be based on the capabilities and skills that have been established in relation to the organizational goals. Powers (1992) suggests that a good selection system must enable the administrator:

- to judge a candidate's skills, knowledge, qualifications, experience, and characteristics
- to match the judgments made to the requirements for the job
- to base their selection decisions on the match between the requirements of the job and the skills, knowledge, qualifications, experiences, and characteristics of the candidates
- to use the information gained in the selection process to initiate development of the selected candidate

The selection of staff process has three interrelated phases (1) before the interview, (2) the interview, and (3) the post interview. Each phase has several actions associated with it. While demonstrating this selection

I. In support of the organizational goals to provide adult basic education (ABE) literacy programs in Palm Beach County, this position exists to deliver educational activities that enable adult learners in the program to perform more effectively in reading and writing.

II. This position is responsible for:

    A. Preparing to instruct
        1. reviewing course content
        2. developing course outline or plan
        3. setting up classroom, equipment, teaching aids, materials and so forth
        4. review class roster
        5. other (please specify) _____

    B. Instructing
        1. use good platform skills
        2. disseminate information in appropriate sequence and manner
        3. employ good questioning techniques
        4. use motivational strategies to enhance learning
        5. other (please specify) _____

    C. Evaluating
        1. evaluate learner performance
        2. evaluate course content
        3. evaluate instructor performance

    D. Updating course materials

    E. Engaging in professional development activities

III. Knowledge, skills, experience, qualifications, and characteristics required or desired for this position:

    A. Knowledge (check all that apply):
       — knowledge of how adults learn
       — knowledge of adults participating in program
       — knowledge of subject matter
       — knowledge of the organizations involved
       — other knowledge required for specific job (please specify) _____

B. Skills (check all that apply)
— climate-setting skills
— verbal skills
— interpersonal skills
— leadership skills
— platform skills
— decision-making skills
— flexibility
— analytical skills
— problem-solving skills
— risk-taking skills
— manage diverse groups
— other skills (please specify) _____

C. Experience (check all that apply)
— skills experience
— technical experience
— teaching experience
— other experiences (please specify) _____

D. Qualifications (check all that apply)
— college degree
— license
— certificate
— train-the-trainer course
— significant instructional experiences
— other qualifications (please specify) _____

E. Characteristics (check all that apply)
— high level energy
— enthusiasm
— strong sense of commitment
— integrity
— ability to model desired behaviors and skills
— self-directed
— ability to seek and accept feedback
— other (please specify) _____

Figure 5.1 Job description and requirements form

process by using the instructor as our illustration, this process can be adapted to other jobs and positions within the agency or organization.

Before the Interview

In this phase you will announce the open position, analyze the candidate data that is forwarded to you, and prepare for the interview itself. You should prepare to write the job announcement based on the job description, skills, and responsibilities you have already defined (see Figure 5.1). By having an accurate and detailed job announcement, it assists interested candidates to assess their candidacy and provides adequate information about the position so they can prepare for an interview. A good announcement should also have, in addition to the job description, other essential information such as salary, work location, work hours, and benefits. The job announcement should also ask candidates to submit evidence that they meet the requirements listed and give them appropriate procedures to follow for submitting such information.

Outlets for announcing job positions can be quite diverse. Where an announcement is placed depends upon several facts such as available resources, type of position, size of organization, and purpose of organization (local, regional, or national in scope). Frequently used approaches for recruiting candidates include placing adds in the local newspaper, trade newsletters and journals, using television and radio spots, distributing job announcement flyers to community-based organizations as well as talking with peers and colleagues in the service area, and finally using an e-mail network (which can be on a local, regional, national, or international scale) to promote the job announcement.

Once the application deadline has passed it is now time to analyze or screen the applications in relationship to the job announcement qualifications. Since you already know the job requirements, a simple selection process could be developed that will allow you to fairly and efficiently evaluate each candidate (see Figure 5.2). In one column list all the job requirements (see Figure 5.1 for list of skills identified).

In the next column write a "R" beside each listed requirement item if it is required for the job or a "D" if it is desired. In the third column list in horizontal fashion the names of the candidates. For each candidate evaluate him or her according to each skill category and its various elements and rate each item as "high", "medium", or "low". After all candidates have been evaluated, the ones with the highest ratings would be selected for personal interviews.

In column 1, list requirements for the job. In column 2, write "R" if item is required, "D" if it is desired. In column 3 write candidates' names and note rating (high, medium, or low) next to each requirement for each candidate.

Rating scale:

High: evidence of substantial knowledge, experience; fully qualified; highly competent in skill areas; desired characteristics judged to be prevalent

Medium: evidence of good knowledge, experience, somewhat qualified; competent in skill areas; desired characteristics judged to be some-what prevalent

Low: evidence of little or no knowledge, experience, qualifications; poor skill; desired characteristics judged to be lacking

Column 1	Column 2	Column 3		
		Name	Name	Name
Knowledge				
1.				
2.				
3.				
4.				
Skills				
1.				
2.				
3.				
4.				
Experience				
1.				
2.				
3.				
4.				
Qualifications				
1.				
2.				
3.				
4.				
Characteristics				
1.				
2.				
3.				
4.				

Figure 5.2 Selection form. Adapted from Powers (1992).

Once you have selected the candidates that will be interviewed, it is a good idea to develop an interview form that will be used during the candidate's interview. The form may have information that reminds you to address such things as (1) welcoming the candidate, (2) describing the purpose of interview, (3) communicating essential information about the job and the agency, (4) listing prior knowledge, qualifications and experience, and asking for verification during the interview, (5) developing certain exercises or hypothetical scenarios that each candidate will be required to address or engage in to demonstrate their strengths in each skill area during the interview process (make notes on the form as to the results or responses), (6) giving the candidate an opportunity to ask questions and to reassess their interest in the job, and (7) thanking the candidate for coming. Each candidate that is interviewed should have an individual interview form developed for him or her.

The Interview

You are now ready to conduct interviews with the selected candidates. If you have developed an interview form the process should be straightforward. After welcoming the candidate, explain the interview process that will be used. During the interview deal with the elements of the job requirements and how the candidate meets them. Address the exercises and hypothetical scenarios developed and make notes on the form. At the end of the interview allow the candidate to ask questions and to give his or her assessment of the position and interest. The final step in the interview is to provide the candidate with a brief but honest assessment of their strengths and weaknesses. Thank the candidate for coming and end the interview.

After the Interview

Selecting the right candidate is difficult, particularly if several candidates are equally qualified. However, if you have developed a good interview form based on the job requirements and skills and have made notes and comments about each candidate the process should be a little easier. You can always find some differences in some of the areas that will separate candidates. When you have made your selection, let the candidate know and explain why he or she was selected. Also address any skill areas that you think need to be improved and developed. Most individuals appreciate the candor, desire, and interest you have expressed in wanting them to be successful. Establish a place and time in which you and the successful candidate can meet to negotiate the final details of the employment agreement.

During this "post interview" phase, you must also contact those candidates who were not selected. It is a good idea to keep the interview forms in case a candidate wants to know why he or she was not selected. If you have taken notes on each candidate, the form will provide adequate feedback to the candidate's inquiry.

DEVELOPING STAFF

A major responsibility you have as an administrator is to communicate what is expected of each staff person and in providing assistance toward the design of a professional development plan. Whether a full-time program coordinator or a part-time ABE instructor, it is important that each and every individual within the agency or organization knows what is expected of them within their respective job positions. Powers (1992) states that "When people don't know what is expected of them, they often spend their time pursuing activities that are not expected (and therefore not valued)" (p. 47). He continues by saying, "A well-defined and clearly communicated set of performance expectations lets people know what accomplishments are important and consequently helps them focus their time and energies on such accomplishments" (p. 48).

Several methods for communicating job expectations can be suggested. The most common is the orientation. Hall (1980) writes that the orientation has three goals: "to help new staff members feel comfortable during their first few days on the job, to teach them the essential routines of the job, and to introduce them to the style of the organization" (p. 203). The orientation process will differ "depending upon the role and place of the new staff member in the hierarchy of the agency" (p. 205); however, the goals of the orientation process are similar at all levels of the agency or organization.

Staff Development Approaches

While the above process assists in orienting individuals, to their role and to the agency, it is staff development activities that help communicate expectations of specific staff positions (Kowalski, 1988; Marsick, 1988;

Smith & Offerman, 1989; Terdy, 1993). If you have developed a job description and responsibilities list for each position in the agency, then an excellent tool for communicating expectations of each position is to refine and extend each major skill area and its related components into a list of standards. For example, an instructor standard under the platform skills category may be "Instructor consistently demonstrates respect toward individual learners." Under each category you may develop 6, 8, or even 10 standards. Sharing standards with each individual according to their position, leaves no doubt what is expected. It allows for an excellent opportunity to dialogue about the expectations and to clarify any concerns and address related questions about their responsibilities.

Another method of staff development is to provide printed materials, such as an employee manual or personnel handbook, to each new employee of the agency or organization. In such printed manuals or handbooks, specific sections may be addressed to specific positions within the agency. For instructors it may address, for example, certain procedures or practices that must be adhered to for classes with potential commercial content such as (1) class time should not be used to overtly and explicitly sell a product or service with which the teacher is associated or can financially benefit from, or (2) literature, including flyers and business cards, that are principally commercially oriented to the teacher's financial interests should not be distributed in class (LERN, 1992). The complete publication entitled "Industry Standards for Classes with Potential Commercial Content" can be obtained by writing to the Learning Resources Network, 1550 Hayes Drive, Manhattan, KS 66502. Good manuals and handbooks can serve as excellent sources for the practical as well as the legal responsibilities that the agency has toward their employees and what the employees have toward the agency.

Internal memoranda is another method toward enhancing the development and information of staff. Knowles (1980) suggests that they can be used to acquaint staff "with new policies, procedures, and activities" (p. 160). Full and part-time staff names should be placed on the mailing list. Many times part-time staff are not kept abreast of new policies, procedures, or events. If you want staff to know what is expected of them, you must communicate that to them and internal memoranda is just one way.

Another staff development mechanism is the staff meeting. These meetings can be used for diverse purposes, from airing concerns to devoting the entire time to specific training needs. While it is difficult to schedule staff meetings, particularly if your agency employees a large percentage of part-time staff such as paid or volunteer instructors, it is important to hold them at least 3 or 4 times per year.

Individual conferences or interviews is another method that can be incorporated into the staff development plan. Knowles (1980, p. 160) states that "following the initial orientation interviews, there should be subsequent interviews-in decreasing frequency" as staff gain experience. Conferences or interviews help staff assess and evaluate their progress toward realizing the expectations of the position.

Professional Development Plan Approaches

In general, an ongoing professional development plan is the responsibility of each individual staff member. Many times, however, new staff need time and guidance provided by the administrator or program director in identifying various strategies for enhancing their professional knowledge and practice bases (Brockett, 1991a). If one purpose of professional development is to help staff critically reflect upon their practice, then several strategies and resources are suggested that will assist them in fulfilling their responsibilities as professionals.

Reading

Whatever the position held within the agency or organization, associated professional literature that is practical as well as theoretical exists. As an administrator you have the opportunity to identify some articles, books, reports, and conference proceedings that address various topics, strategies, processes, and information outlets that will be useful for specific staff. Brockett (1991b) states that among the "potential benefits of reading professional literature are (1) developing new knowledge; (2) sharing new information and ideas; (3) promoting critical thinking; and (4) fostering professional socialization and reaffirmation" (p. 195). It is important for you to encourage your staff to engage in reading professional literature. To start the process, you may want to make copies of specific journal articles you have found helpful in your practice and share them with the instructors. Perhaps in a later interview or conference with individual staff, you can discuss the impressions or ideas generated from the readings.

Journal Writing

Regardless of the staff position held, keeping a journal is an important component of the critical reflection process. As Brockett (1991b) states, "by putting our thoughts down on paper, a lasting record of thoughts, feelings, and ideas has been created" (p. 197). One approach to journal writing is to have four or five questions that you address after each day's work such as, "What actions, comments, or gestures delighted you most and why?"; "What actions, comments or gestures discouraged you the most and why?"; "When did you feel most affirmed today and why?"; "When did you feel most distanced and why?"; "What insights did you realize about your position that surprised you the most and why?". Staff journals can be shared, if the author wishes to do so, with you. Otherwise it should serve as a private account of one's ideas, feelings, and thoughts and over time a reflection of how staff has come to understand their professional practice.

Professional Associations and Conferences

Another expectation you, as the administrator, should hold is that your staff should belong to appropriate professional associations and attend their conferences. Professional associations exist on the local, state/provincial, regional, national, and international levels. Darkenwald and Merriam (1982) suggests that opportunities for professional development may be the single most important function of associations. By joining professional associations, you usually receive journals, magazines, newsletters, and various conference and book announcements. Perhaps most importantly it demonstrates a commitment you have for the field. Administrators should lead by example!

Conferencing can be a valuable professional development experience. Benefits of attending conferences include opportunities to network with others who share common interests concerns, to learn about new practices and to share innovative ideas that you have generated, to formally present your ideas and experiences in a conference session, and to validate your professional purpose.

In-Service Activities

Organizations should make provisions for in-service training. Larger organizations may develop a schedule of diverse offerings to meet the ever-changing professional needs of their staff. Smaller organizations may develop and offer certain training but may need to work cooperatively with related agencies on an agreement that would allow their staff to participate in in-service activities provided by the cooperating agency. In-service activities are excellent professional development tools if designed properly. Usually, such activities are very focused and much can be accomplished in a short time period, if a good instructor is present.

Electronic Networking

As technology expands, electronic networks become a more feasible dimension of everyone's professional development process. Accessibility to a computer, modem, and an electronic network can provide to each staff member the opportunity to communicate with others locally, nationally, and internationally. Electronic networking increases the potential network of professionals who share common concerns, ideas, and responsibilities as well as perhaps common solutions to certain program problems (Knox, 1993). With the increase in technological advances, small and large agencies and organizations will have the opportunity to engage in electronic networking in a cost-efficient manner. Because of that, staff members should be encouraged to incorporate into their professional development plan the use of electronic networking.

Credit and Noncredit Courses

There are many opportunities to enroll in noncredit as well as credit courses that are offered by community-based organizations, public schools, community colleges, and regional and state universities, in an effort to enhance your professional development plan. Taking courses has a number of potential benefits such as (1) exposure to some of the most recent thinking and research, (2) opportunities to establish informal and formal networks, and 3) potential for new professional opportunities. There are always new and better ways, strategies, and processes for meeting professional duties and responsibilities that ultimately lead to enhancing professional practice. Taking courses is just another approach that administrators can encourage their staff to engage in and make part of their professional development plan.

SUMMARY

Selecting and developing paid and volunteer staff is an important function of your administrative duties. Selecting staff in a fair, equitable, and professional manner will depend upon how well you have defined the job description, articulated and identified the job roles and responsibilities, and developed a system for selecting qualified and skilled candidates.

Strategies for accomplishing these tasks are provided. Communicating the expectations of the job to respective staff is also an essential function as well as assisting in the creation of effective staff development strategies. Several approaches were suggested that should be vital components of any professional development plan.

CHAPTER 6

Marketing and Public Relations

The success and effectiveness of adult, community, and continuing education programs in organizations depend greatly upon how well the two important ingredients of marketing and public relations are understood and implemented. To secure a competitive edge in the market of potential learners within the community, administrators must possess a basic understanding of the concepts, principles, and implementation strategies associated with marketing and public relations.

The majority of this chapter will be dedicated to the discussion of marketing, the elements of a marketing plan, and promotional strategies for marketing your programs with emphasis on direct-mail marketing. In addition, a brief examination on how to develop effective brochures will be presented. The remainder of the chapter will present information and strategies for effective public relations.

MARKETING

How is marketing defined? Rados (1981) defines marketing as follows: "Marketing. . . . deals with the many methods by which A tries to get B to do his will, where B has freedom to act as he chooses" (p. 17). Kotler (1984) defines marketing as "a social process by which individuals and groups obtain what they need and want through creating and exchanging products and value with others" (p. 4). Marketing is, among other things, according to Beder (1986), "a methodology for attracting learners, a methodology that guides program development, promotion, pricing, distribution and market research. . . . " (p. 3). Gilley and Eggland (1992) suggest that marketing is "a technique used to improve or enhance the image of products, services, or an organization" (p. 4). Bryan (1993) notes that marketing is the offering of something of value to someone in exchange for something else of value.

While a number of approaches exist for viewing marketing such as the traditional model, the exchange model, and the adaptive model, it is the exchange model put forth by Kotler (1984) that many adult, community, and continuing education organizations subscribe. The exchange model suggests that the organization establishes a symbiotic relationship with consumers. In this relationship, as described by Simerly (1989a), a constant negotiation, trading, and information-sharing process is going on that ultimately leads to some sort of decision making. The guiding force of the exchange model is that "consumers are asked to exchange something of value (for example money or time) for something they perceive as a benefit (for example, programs, products, and services). The exchange approach to marketing focuses on consumers and the sponsoring organization exchanging things they each value" (p. 7).

While it is impossible to detail in depth all the concepts and principles of the practice of marketing because of space limitations, many excellent books exist that will assist in enhancing your conceptual as well as practical understanding. Providing excellent coverage on marketing for profit and nonprofit adult, community, and continuing education organizations are books by Beder (1986), Gilley and Eggland (1992), Kotler (1984, 1986), Kotler and Andreasen (1987), Simerly (1990), and Simerly and Associates (1989). Each book discusses many facets of marketing, including how to develop a marketing plan. It is to this element of the marketing process we now turn.

Developing a Marketing Plan

The marketing plan is an integral part of the broader strategic planning process (see Chapter 2). Walshok (1987) notes that "in the last decade of increasing competition for members, clients, and students, leaders in the not-for-profit sector have come to rely increasingly on marketing activities and marketing strategies. . . . " (p. 149). In this section we will examine briefly the six stages of a marketing plan.

Stage 1

In many cases, the adult, community, or continuing education program is part of a larger organization, for example a religious institution, a public school district, or a community college or university. Therefore, the first stage of a marketing plan is to clarify the parent organization's mission and constituencies and to determine its broader goals and objectives. Once the parent organization's mission is understood in terms of what the organization does, what it is known for, and the sorts of societal needs it is committed to serving, your program mission and constituencies are more easily identified (Walshok, 1987). Beder (1986) states:

> Clarity of mission is important because lack of clarity may have two unfortunate consequences. First, programs developed will lack coherence and participation, and income will suffer. Second, and ultimately more important, the continuing education unit will soon find itself at odds with its parent institution as it develops programs that conflict with the larger institution's philosophy. (p. 4)

In the same vein of thought, Foster (1989a) suggests that "an organization should set realistic goals in line with what the institution really is before setting marketing goals and objectives" (p. 50).

Stage 2

The second stage is to develop your program's marketing mission. In relation to the parent organization, Gilley and Eggland (1992) ask you to consider the following questions as you develop a marketing mission:

- What is our purpose?
- Who are our constituencies/clients?
- What do we have that is valuable to our constituencies/clients?
- What should our purpose be?
- What will our purpose be in the future?

In addition, Gilley and Eggland suggest that "A well-developed mission statement gives everyone in the organization a sense of purpose, direction, significance, and achievement" (p. 76).

Stage 3

The next stage is to analyze the various factors that affect your program's ability to market educational programs. Social, cultural, economic, geographical, or political variables influence the attendant environment and basically charts the direction for your marketing process. Gilley and Eggland (1992) state, "Marketing, by its very nature, requires interactions with assorted situational elements that must be accounted for in the process of marketing planning" (p. 78). Analyzing these various factors assist you, the administrator, in determining the opportunities and constraints your program may be confronted with in its efforts to market educational programs. Foster (1989a) has identified some of these variables and places them under the headings of "macroenvironmental factors" and "microenvironmental factors" (p. 54).

Macroenvironmental factors are global trends in such areas as demographics (i.e., aging of the baby boom population, increased number of women in the workplace, geographic population shifts), economics (i.e., forecasted information on U.S. and world economies, forecasted slow growth rate and high interest rates in U.S. economy), technology (i.e., emergence of technologies providing for teacher-student interaction from remote classrooms, gradual acceptance of television as an educational medium), and politics (i.e., the move to decentralization and its effect on monitoring education, the move toward more lean, measurably cost-effective educational organizations). Macroenvironmental factors help us see "the big picture" and provides us with images of how it may effect the marketing process of our adult, community, and continuing education programs.

Microenvironmental factors are more localized in nature and are concerned with the same variables mentioned above, demographics, economics, politics, and technology, but from your situation-specific perspective. For example, the demographics in your community may be shifting to an older mean age; economically the local community is experiencing a high rate of unemployment and business and industry closings; politically, newly elected officials hold a philosophy that education is for the young and not for adults; and finally, technologically, the delivery of programs must be adjusted to the new mediums available. Paying attention to the macro and microenvironmental factors may assist in determining the feasibility of accomplishing the marketing mission.

Stage 4

Now that you have recognized the possibility that the elements of the exchange model exist, the next stage is to engage in the process of market segmentation. According to Beder (1986), market segmentation "is a process of dividing the potential market into subgroups according to how they are expected to react to program offerings" (p. 7). Gilley and Eggland (1992) define *market* as "a universe of people who have an actual or potential interest in a product or service and the ability to pay for that product or service" (p. 99). The idea behind market segmentation is that constituencies' or clients' preferences are often clustered, and through market segmentation procedures the existence of natural market segments can be revealed, can be used to construct market segments, or can reveal the lack of any market segments (Gilley & Eggland, 1992).

Market segmentation has no established formula, although three kinds of variables are typically used in segmenting consumer markets: geographic, demographic, and psychographic. Geographic variables include such things as dividing the market by location such as a neighborhood or the geographical distance of potential learners from the program location. Demographic variables are sex, age, family size, income, education level, nationality, and occupation. Psychographic variables relate to individual behavior patterns such as lifestyle and personality. This is also referred to as behavioristic segmentation and many believe the psychographic or behavioristic variables are the best starting point for constructing effective market segments (Gilley & Eggland, 1992).

Stage 5

The fifth stage in the marketing plan is to determine what kind of targeting strategy will be used to market the program. Three strategies could be used. The first is *undifferentiated marketing* which is mass marketing. Lower costs result from this type of marketing as well as reduced constituencies' satisfaction of meeting individual needs. If one segment is selected as the focus of its marketing efforts this is referred to as *concentrated marketing*. Higher risk is involved in this strategy, according to Beder (1986), but it can be effective if your program "is relatively new and lacks the resources to serve more than one segment" (p. 8). The third strategy is *differentiated marketing* which operates in two or more segments of the market but has separate programs for each segment. Generally speaking, this approach produces the best results and the best service to your clientele. Gilley and Eggland (1992) note that marketing segmentation and the appropriately selected marketing strategy can help administrators determine which clients need specific education programs and services, and they can offer evidence on the depth and breadth of a population and its interest in education.

Stage 6

The sixth stage is concerned with determining the proper marketing mix of product, pricing, and place—once the educational unit has identified the segments of its potential market in which it may serve. Riggs (1989) suggests that decisions about adult, community, and continuing education products "should focus on the programs, goods, and services offered for sale" (p. 126). She continues by stating that "A product must be defined in terms of the benefits to the buyer. The critical question that organizations must ask is, 'What is the buyer buying?' Once that question is answered, the next step is to define what is being sold and to state the product in terms of its benefits to customers" (p. 126). Within this product decision-making process, the administrator must decide what tangible core product will stand at the center of the organization's product line. Core products motivate participation. For example, when learners participate in a Lamaze class, the core product is enhanced knowledge and less anxiety during child birth. When college professors participate in a continuing education course on mentoring, the core product is improved instructional and advisory skills and enhanced personal relationships.

The next aspect of the marketing mix is pricing. Beder (1986) suggests that pricing is "a vital function of marketing, not only because price is a critical element of exchange but also because price in relation to participation level determines the income of the continuing education unit" (p. 15). The first step is to determine objectives for pricing and to consider all pricing strategies and alternatives (Riggs, 1989). Kotler (1986) places pricing into three major categories: cost-oriented, demand-oriented, and competition-oriented. *Cost-oriented pricing* means prices are set largely on the basis of cost, including overhead (Riggs, 1989). *Demand-oriented pricing* is determined on the basis of demand rather than cost, that is the adult, community, or continuing education unit charges what the market will bear. For example, a higher pricing structure may be set for industry because they can afford to pay more versus a lower pricing structure set for the public sector, who usually demands lower pricing if they are to participate. *Competition-oriented pricing*, which is the most popular type of pricing, means the adult, community, or continuing education unit charges what the competition charges. Pricing of programs are not too high nor too low in relation to the competitions, but usually at the average relative to the competition (Riggs, 1989).

A well-designed product and pricing mix will not be successful unless the markets are aware of the next component of the marketing mix—place. Place relates to location of your educational offerings. Several aspects of place must be considered such as what are the tangible benefits of location—design of facilities, comfort and amenities, and convenience—against the cost and expenditures involved in getting to the location. Basically, know what your constituencies are accustomed to and do not locate programs in places that will disenchant them.

Developing a marketing plan is not an easy task but it is an essential one if your educational unit is going to be competitive and understands the needs, wants, and preferences of your constituencies. We have presented a marketing plan that is comprised of six stages: (1) clarify parent organization's mission and constituencies, (2) develop programs marketing mission, (3) analyze environmental factors, (4) engage in market segmentation, (5) determine target strategies, and (6) decide the proper marketing mix. For more specifics and details on how to develop an integrated marketing and advertising plan as well as see a sample of such a plan, we encourage you to read Foster (1989a; 1989b). A marketing plan, which includes an effective marketing mix, that leads to well-designed educational programs will not be successful unless the markets are aware of it, informed on what it is suppose to do for them, and have some idea of where or how to obtain it. It is at this point administrators must recognize the importance of communicating and promoting their programs.

Marketing Your Programs

In this section we will discuss some promotional aspects of marketing your program by examining briefly direct-mail marketing, selecting mailing lists, and brochure development. For more in-depth reading on these areas see Simerly (1990) and Simerly and Associates (1989).

Direct-Mail Marketing

Direct-mail marketing is the primary form of promotion used by adult, community, and continuing education organizations because it outperforms newspaper and magazine ads, radio/television commercials, outdoor signs, yellow pages, and package inserts. Elliott (1989) notes that educators choose direct-mail marketing to increase registrations for several reasons: (1) it is "usually the most cost-effective technique because it yields a higher response relative to cost than any other advertising medium", (2) it "permits selectivity"—that is "the flexibility to target mailings makes it possible to select market segments that are likely to respond to a continuing education program offer", and (3) "it allows you to tailor the promotional message . . . [and] can be used to send a personalized message" (p. 141). However, to be successful at direct-mail marketing you must know how to find and select mailing lists that get results.

The most used source of mailing list information is the Standard Rate and Data Service's Direct Mail List Rates and Data. This quarterly catalogue provides complete lists of names, addresses, and phone numbers of listing houses. For more information write or call:

Direct Mail List Rates and Data
Standard Rate and Data Service, Inc.
3004 Glenview Road
Wilmette, IL 60091
(312) 256-6067

It is good practice to establish an ongoing relationship with three or four list houses "so they can get to know the special needs of your organization and its programs. In this way they will be better able to serve your special list selection needs on a continuing basis" (Simerly, 1990, p. 33).

Andrew (1989) suggests that the type of lists you choose "depends on your audience, advertising objectives, and budget" (p. 179). In general, the two most common types of lists are the house lists and outside lists. *House lists* contain names of individuals who have participated in activities of your organization. *Outside lists* contain names of those who have not participated in your organization's educational offerings. House lists can be a very valuable source of information if you learn how to profile your present customers and use this data to target your mailings. For example, you can take the names of all participants and code their information into areas such as geographic, demographic, psychographic, and behavioristic. From these constructed profiles of potential customers the response and participation rate should increase. You also need to know which mailing list is getting the best return. You can do this through the process of tracking a key-code number, symbol, or some other identifiable source that is placed on the registration form. Andrew states "mailing efficiency means greater response at lower costs" (p. 185).

The outside list contains names and profiles of potential clients for your educational program offerings. Lists obtained through list houses are usually rented and not purchased. Therefore, since list houses are in the business of making a profit, it is illegal to make a copy of any rented list. To obtain the most cost-effective and ultimately the most profitable return on your investment, it is a good policy to use a list broker who knows your business and market and can "compare many lists from many different companies and recommend the ones most appropriate for your particular needs" (Andrew, 1989, p. 185). According to Simerly (1990) suggests working with a list broker has many advantages such as:

- It saves time. They shop for lists for you.
- It saves money. Because of their extensive contacts, they can usually obtain the best lists at the best rates.
- They act as your direct-mail expert consultant and make recommendations on compiling a mailing list based on the individual needs of your particular advertising project.
- They have no allegiance to any single list house or association. Therefore, they will often recommend lists from several different sources as being best for meeting your needs.
- List brokers usually receive a commission of 15 to 20 percent of the cost of the list rental. However, the list house from which the list is rented pays this commission rather than you having to pay it. Thus, using the help of a professional list broker does not cost you any more than doing all of this yourself.

In addition to using a list broker to secure appropriate lists, you can obtain many lists free from various organizations and associations.

As with house lists, outside lists can be profiled so certain information can be obtained for specific target mailings. You should also consider a merge/purge. In this process "tapes of house and outside lists are run against each other to eliminate duplicates, update addresses, and identify nixies" (Andrew, 1989, p. 187). To secure insights as which mail lists are receiving the most response, it is essential to engage in the process of tracking through coding the registration forms. Simerly (1990) provides a checklist that "summarizes the major items to include in an effective system for mailing list selection, maintenance, and tracking" (p. 58). That checklist is reproduced here in Figure 6.1. For additional practical information on the direct-mail marketing, we recommend reading Elliott (1989), Andrew (1989), and Simerly (1990).

Developing Effective Brochures

Whether you are the administrator of a large adult, community, or continuing education organization or a small one, direct-mail brochures will be the primary means of publicizing your program offerings. Simerly (1989b) states that "no matter what the size of the continuing education organization, the principles of writing effective copy for brochures are the same" (p. 166). He suggests that brochures are divided into "the front cover, introduction/background, who should attend, special features,

The following checklist summarizes the major items to include in an effective system for mailing list selection, maintenance, and tracking. Review and modify this list to meet the specific needs of your organization. Then it can form the basis for an effective, ongoing check system.

List Rental Issues

_____ 1. Have lists been rented from a reliable list source such as a professional list house?

_____ 2. Have you secured mailing lists from professional associations as appropriate?

_____ 3. Have you avoided making unauthorized copies of lists?

_____ 4. Have you employed the services of a professional, reliable list broker as appropriate?

_____ 5. Have you considered renting lists from the Yellow Pages of the phone directory?

_____ 6. Have you checked the data card for each list to ensure that the list meets your specific needs?

Acquiring Additional Lists

_____ 7. Have you used reliable sources to obtain appropriate free lists, such as local civic and business clubs?

_____ 8. Have you considered conducting a survey as a means of acquiring mailing lists?

Merge/Purge Issues

_____ 9. Have you considered running a merge/purge for large mailings?

_____ 10. If you do not run a merge/purge, have you arranged to stagger mailings on different days to avoid having recipients receive more than one copy of a brochure on the same day?

Mailing List Format

_____ 11. Have you chosen Cheshire or Avery labels as appropriate for the needs of your mailing?

_____ 12. Have you ordered all labels with the nine-digit zip code rather than just the five-digit zip code?

_____ 13. Have you ordered all labels separated by zip code?

Maintaining Mailing Lists

_____ 14. Have you created a simple way to update all your internal mailing lists?

_____ 15. Have you created an internal, preferred mailing list of important opinion makers who need to receive your mailings even if they are not necessarily candidates to attend a program themselves?

Coding and Tracking Mailing Lists

_____ 16. Have you ordered all rented lists with a code on each label for effective tracking?

_____ 17. Do large lists have appropriate subcategories with separate tracking codes?

_____ 18. Is the registration form designed to capture the mailing list code for each registrant regardless of where the registration form appears in your advertising?

_____ 19. Have you designed a special tracking system for securing the mailing list for all phone registrations?

_____ 20. Have you designed a special tracking system to track the mail and phone responses for all newspaper and magazine ads?

_____ 21. Have you designed a spreadsheet on a personal computer to help analyze the cost benefit for your marketing activities for individual programs?

_____ 22. Have you developed a system to capture the names and addresses of everyone who phones in for information about any program?

Figure 6.1 Checklist for mailing list selection, maintenance, and tracking. Permission to reproduce granted in R. G. Simerly (1990). *Planning and marketing conferences and workshops: Tips, tools, and techniques.* San Francisco: Jossey-Bass.

program content, presenter's biographies, general information, and back cover" (p. 167). In general brochures should never be smaller than 8 1/2 × 11 inches in size. The size is important because it gives you the space necessary to accomplish the information goals you have developed. As Simerly (1989b) suggests, we are conditioned to the 8 1/2 × 11 inch size and "anything smaller may be lost on the desk of a busy person. Or even worse, smaller brochures may look less important and tend to be ignored by readers" (p. 167).

Let's look briefly at the various components of brochures and ask ourselves some questions. The front cover has the sole purpose of attracting attention and encouraging the reader to open the brochure and read its contents. Here are some questions put forth by Simerly (1989c) concerning the front cover. Does the title accurately describe the program? Is the front cover bold? Is the title large and eye catching? Do the dates appear on the cover? Does the story begin on the cover or are teasers used effectively?

The next part of the brochure is the introduction/background statement which should be designed to "(1) further establish the image of a quality program, (2) provide the necessary background to tell why the program is being presented, (3) generate enough interest to encourage the reader to read all of the copy, and (4) enhance the credibility of the program" (Simerly, 1989b, p. 167). Questions about this part may include: Does this statement help set the tone for the entire program? Does the introduction/background provide a natural lead-in to the comprehensive description of the program content?

Who should attend is the next part of the brochure that should be addressed. It is important to spell out clearly who your program is designed for and why. Presented in the brochure should be a comprehensive outline of the program content as well. The program content should be written in a clear and concise manner that provides enough information to readers to convince them the program is appropriate for them. The program content section, "next to the front cover, is probably the single most critical area in the brochure" (Simerly, 1989b, p. 170).

The special features section of the brochure emphasizes the uniqueness of the program. Have you spelled them out clearly for the reader? Special features may constitute brief descriptions of what opportunities they will experience, how they will be provided with special written handouts, or how they will have the opportunity to meet and discuss face to face with well-known personalities in their field.

Another dimension of the brochure is to provide a good biographical copy which should, as Simerly (1989b) suggests, "legitimize the expertise of presenters so that readers will say, Yes, that's a person who has good credentials, experience, and expertise. I could learn a lot from this person. I ought to attend the program" (p. 173). A question you may ask is, does the biographical copy encourage the reader to attend in order to learn from an expert?

The next section of the brochure is for general information. It contains all the important information participants need to register. Simerly (1989c) provides some excellent checklist questions. Have you included three easy ways to register—by phone, by fax, and by mail? Are the time and location given so that people do not wonder where and when to show up? Is the information on fees correct and clear? Are the options of registering by credit card, being billed, or submitting a purchase order offered? Are the name and telephone number of the person to contact for additional information given? Are registration times listed? Are beginning and ending times for the program stated? Is information about meals and other social events included? Is appropriate information about hotel reservations included? Is the refund policy clearly stated? Is there a clearly designed registration form?

The last part of the brochure is the back cover which has several important purposes—provides a place for a mailing label and a logo, and contains the general information and registration form. Checklist questions include: Is the back cover treated as valuable advertising space? Have the title, dates, and sponsorship for the program been listed? Is the back cover bold enough to invite the reader to pick up the brochure and read it?

Simerly (1989c) provides an excellent checklist for direct-mail brochures that we encourage you to review as you develop brochure copy for your program. He also encourages adult, community, and continuing education administrators to set up a production schedule for their direct-mail marketing process. Usually, you should give yourself 4 months for the development of program copy until the brochures are in the mailboxes of prospective registrants. Two and a half months are usually spent working with graphic designers, typesetters, and printers on the development of the brochure. The brochures you send out announcing educational offerings establishes your image, good or bad, as a organization. Simerly (1990) provides an excellent checklist for establishing quality and excellence in graphic design, typesetting, and printing, which is reproduced in Figure 6.2. In this checklist, it provides more specifics on such things as typeface and size, color of ink, artwork, photographs, and paper

As you review this list, modify it to include all the essential elements you need to consider for producing excellence in graphic design, typesetting, and printing.

Working with a Graphic Designer

_____ 1. Employ a professional graphic designer for your advertising projects.

_____ 2. Secure a letter of agreement from the graphic designer stating the terms and services to be provided for each project.

_____ 3. Consider using your graphic designer for a wide variety of services such as taking projects to the typesetter and printer and proofing copy.

_____ 4. Build a long-term relationship with several graphic designers.

Issues Related to Typeface and Size

_____ 5. Use a minimum of different type faces within any one advertising piece.

_____ 6. Decide whether serif or sans-serif type is most appropriate.

_____ 7. Use 10- or 12-point type for the bulk of copy text, preferably 12-point.

_____ 8. Be sure that the general information section that contains information about times, place, price, and how to register is in type that can be easily read, even by people with bifocals.

Choosing Colors of Ink

_____ 9. The bulk of all text copy in a direct-mail brochure should be black or dark blue for the easiest readability.

_____ 10. Do not use yellow ink for copy! It "bleeds" and cannot be read easily.

_____ 11. Avoid other light pastel inks for copy.

_____ 12. Avoid metallic colored ink for large blocks of text.

_____ 13. Avoid reversing out large blocks of text.

_____ 14. A good alternative to reverse-outs for large blocks of text is screening at 10 or 20 percent.

_____ 15. Using more than one color of ink is usually not the critical variable that will increase registrations.

_____ 16. To save money, work with your graphic designer to find creative ways to create the illusion that more than one color of ink has been used.

Using Photographs and Artwork

_____ 17. Employ a professional photographer for producing quality pictures in all advertising.

_____ 18. Always create a mixture of males and females in pictures if your target audience contains males and females.

_____ 19. Always consider the cultural diversity of your target audience and reflect this in all photographs.

_____ 20. Be sure to use current photographs.

_____ 21. Always order high-contrast, glossy prints from the photograph processor.

Choosing Paper Stock

_____ 22. Select paper stock that compliments the image and quality of your program.

_____ 23. White or buff-colored paper provides the best background for easy-to-read printing.

Working with a Typesetter and Printer

_____ 24. Save money by arranging with your typesetter to receive copy on a computer disk. This avoids having to rekey text.

_____ 25. Be sure that everyone agrees to all corrections on copy before any of it goes to the graphic designer.

_____ 26. Never produce any direct-mail brochure that is smaller than 8 1/2 by 11 inches.

_____ 27. Always get competitive bids for each project before selecting a printer.

_____ 28. Carefully review as many bluelines as necessary to guarantee a flawless final printed product.

_____ 29. If you receive inferior work from any printer, ask to have your job reprinted at the printer's expense.

_____ 30. Institute your own checking procedures to ensure quality control on all jobs. For example, check every hundredth item.

Figure 6.2 Checklist for establishing quality and excellence in graphic design, typesetting, and printing. Permission to reproduce granted in R. G. Simerly (1990). *Planning and marketing conferences and workshops: Tips, tools, and techniques.* San Francisco: Jossey-Bass.

stock. This checklist can be adapted to meet your individual organizational needs.

Utilizing the checklists provided in this chapter should assist and encourage you and your staff to think strategically about the various dimensions of direct-mail marketing.

PUBLIC RELATIONS

Public relations is the process of promoting the image and goodwill of your adult, community, or continuing education organization. Patterson (1989) states that "public relations is a complex series of tools, techniques, activities, and strategies that educate the public about an organization" (p. 203). In addition, it is an essential function of the administrator. While most adult, community, and continuing education organizations do not have full-time public relation specialists, organizational administrators many times must be "the primary promoter, press agent, lobbyist, image shaper, opinion influencer, and public relations campaigner in addition to their many other responsibilities" (Patterson, 1989, p. 201). In this section, the elements of a public relations plan will be examined and some strategies for promoting your program will be presented.

The Public Relations Plan

Public relations is an essential component and function of the marketing plan. Gilley (1989) suggests that adult, community, and continuing education organizations, "like individuals, develop a personality or image over time. . . . The way a particular education organization is perceived by the public is important because it helps determine consumer acceptance of the organization's programs and services" (p. 216). He continues by noting that the image people have of an organization influences all aspects of its operation. Therefore, it seems imperative that a public relations plan be development that will reflect the image of the organization, and its products, programs, and services. A public relations plan can consist of the following elements: (1) defining the mission statement, (2) determining program goals, (3) analyzing publics, (4) identifying benefits to the constituencies, and (5) deciding on public relations strategies. Each of these components will be briefly examined.

Defining the Mission Statement

The first essential element of the public relations plan is to define the adult, community, or continuing education organization's role within the parent organization or within the community. What makes your program unique? What is your organization's purpose and how does that purpose make you unique among your competitors? As in the marketing plan, your mission statement and the public relations position taken should not be in conflict with the parent organization or with the image the community holds about your organization.

Determining the Goals

What should be the goals of the public relation plan? How will these goals lead to strategies for accomplishing your plan? In determining goals it is essential to address such questions as who are our constituencies for the various activities we offer? Why do they enroll in the programs, use the services, or desire the products? What is the image of the program in the community? What is the organization's reputation?

Ultimately you want to wrestle with these questions and write them as goal statements. How do you want our program image to be perceived in the community? What kind of reputation is desired? How can publicity strategies contribute to our efforts to enhance our image and reputation (Patterson, 1989)?

Analyzing Our Constituents

A public relations plan must be focused to the individuals your organization believes are potential program, product, or services users. The process explained earlier concerning market segmentation is relevant here as well as in analyzing your constituents. It is essential to understand and know your constituents' markets. Considering all the programs and services your program offers, it is important to determine the ideal user's profile. Are they male or female? What is their age range? Where do they live? What are their incomes and levels of education? Since you want to engage in a public relations strategy, you must determine what forms of media they utilize—radio, television, newspaper, magazines, newsletters. Do they read direct-mail brochures, letters, or pamphlets? Do they utilize various electronic networks? Knowing and analyzing your constituents will assist in the development of a focused public relations plan.

Benefits to the Constituencies

Why should the identified constituents invest their time, money, and energy in your program offerings? What's in it for them? If you have determined and analyzed your constituents correctly, you will know what media forms they interact with and what groups you need to focus on for your public relations campaign. Ultimately, this information will assist in selecting and designing the correct activities, tools, strategies, and techniques to accomplish the goals of your plan.

Deciding on the Strategies

The strategies you select are directly related to what goals you have established for the program. If you had a goal to increase the revenues of the program by 5 percent over a 1 year period, then a public relations strategy to reach that goal may include being involved in three radio interviews during the year. The strategies you select should be designed to reach your target audience to enhance the image of the organization. There are many diverse tools and strategies available. In the next section we will examine some of them.

Public Relations Strategies and Tools

There are a number of strategies and tools to consider in the development of a public relations plan. Patterson (1989) provides a list of various types of public relations strategies to achieve the plan:

1. Electronic media, commercial, or public broadcasts
   — Computers, on-line access
   — Movies
   — Networks
   — Radio shows
   — Slide shows
   — Television shows
   — Videotapes
   — Video text monitors

2. News conferences

3. Press kits

4. Public gatherings
   — Advisory committees
   — Ceremonies
   — Exhibitions
   — Lectures and seminars
   — Trade shows

5. Public service announcements

6. Publications
   — Annual reports
   — Books, brochures, and bulletins
   — Calendars of events
   — Catalogues
   — Financial reports
   — Handbooks
   — Inserts in mailers
   — Magazines
   — Newsletters

7. Publicity releases
   — Announcements
   — Feature articles
   — Interviews
   — White papers

8. Speakers' bureau

9. Special events

10. Volunteer, support, and/or advisory groups

Let's look at several of these strategies and tools in more detail.

News Releases

News releases can be utilized by the various forms of media such as newspapers, radio, and television. Gilley (1989) notes that a well-written news release has six components: who, what, when, where, why, and how. It should provide the reader with all the essential information about the program or service offered by the educational organization. He suggests that in addition, "the name, title, address, and telephone number of the individual to call or write regarding the story should be provided" (p.

222). This form of publicity is very informative and usually free of cost to your organization. However, you also have little control over when it will be printed or aired.

Speakers' Bureau

A speakers' bureau is comprised of staff, advisory, and volunteer committee members who could appear for radio and television interviews and speak at various organizations and community groups about your organization. You may develop a slide show or a videotape that demonstrates the value and commitment to the community and shows how your organization meets the needs of learners. Know what you want to accomplish through your speakers' bureau activities. Notify chambers of commerce and civic, social, service, cultural, fraternal, and professional organizations that your staff is available for speeches, interviews, and presentations.

Public Service Announcements

Patterson (1989) states that "radio and television stations often run free public service announcements related to upcoming events. Although there is no regulation requiring them to run these public service announcements, many of them do so as a means of providing service to the community" (p. 212). These announcements are brief, factual statements 30 to 60 seconds long and are used to highlight your organization or special event. Public service announcements are prepared like news releases. The upside of public service announcements as a public relations tool is that they are free. However, the negative side is they are rarely broadcast in prime time; consequently, they reach the late night or early morning listener or viewer most often.

Active Membership in Community Organizations

Being involved in community organizations, especially volunteer leadership roles, is a good public relations strategy. It provides high visibility to your program through the networking process. Patterson (1989) says you should "seek collaboration opportunities with appropriate groups to multiply publicity efforts. Participating in leadership of community organizations can be one of your most effective strategies for developing effective public relations" (p. 212).

Special Events

Special events can be organized that will gain recognition and attention for your organization. Whatever special event is chosen be sure it carries the appropriate message for the targeted audience. There is a wide variety of types of special events that can be used in this public relations process such as:

- Auctions
- Awards
- Bazaars
- Benefits
- Contests
- Dinners
- Displays
- Exhibits
- Fairs
- Lectures
- Membership Drives
- Parades
- Open Houses/Receptions
- Rummage sales
- Seminars
- Symposiums
- Volunteer day
- Workshops

Whichever special event you engage in, be sure that it is well planned and that all details such as budget, timing, facilities, and location have been carefully considered and carried out.

Publishing Articles

One of the most overlooked form of publicity is getting published in trade and professional journals. When you consider that most journal articles published have the author's name, position/title, and affiliation/organization, it is a very effective forum for enhancing the image of the author as well as the identity of the organization (Gilley, 1989). It is important to understand some rules of the publishing process. As a result you must develop a strategic approach to getting published. What kind of article do you want to write—practitioner or research? Who is the target audience or readership? Have you selected the most appropriate journal or magazine? Have you discussed the article contents with colleagues? Have you talked with an editor about your idea? Do you know about editorial policies and style? Can you develop a professional and attractive manuscript?

Seeking answers to these questions are helpful, especially if this is your beginning efforts at getting published. Writing articles for publication should be a professionally and personally rewarding experience, therefore, seek some assistance from colleagues who have published and know the process. While journal and magazine publishing is a somewhat overlooked publicity strategy, it is a valuable process to enhance the image of your organization.

SUMMARY

Marketing and public relation efforts are essential to the success of any adult, community, and continuing education organization. When we recognize the fact that our viability as an organization depends upon promoting our programs, services, or products successfully, the importance of being informed about marketing and public relations becomes quite evident. As an administrator, it is imperative that you are actively engaged in the planning and implementation processes of marketing and public relations.

The previous chapters have discussed some essential administrative functions and tasks. How successful these functions and tasks are realized depends upon the administrator's ability to utilize evaluative processes. The next chapter will examine the topic of evaluation.

CHAPTER 7

Evaluating Programs

Evaluation is an essential element in effective programs for any target group. The recent emphasis on accountability and restructuring (Minzey & LeTarte, 1994), combined with funding cuts, requires administrators of all types of educational enterprises not only to provide documentation of results, but also to do more with less. As they struggle to determine the best use of resources, many have developed a greater appreciation of the role evaluation can play in identifying problem areas and testing alternative approaches.

One motivation for administrators of programs for adults to carefully plan and implement evaluation is a drive toward excellence, the desire to continually seek ways to improve every aspect of the program; the other is survival. In most adult programs, participation is voluntary, and if their needs are not being met, adult learners will "vote with their feet" and go elsewhere.

As discussed in Chapter 3, evaluation should be an integral part of the planning process at both the program level and the course level, taking place on an ongoing basis as well as at the end of specified offerings or time periods. While the adult education administrator is, of course, responsible for the evaluation at both levels, actual involvement in the planning and implementation will naturally be greater at the program level. The administrator's role in course level evaluation is normally focused on ensuring that procedures and guidelines related to the gathering of evaluative data are in place. A third major area of evaluation which requires the attention of the adult education administrator is the assessment of the effectiveness of learning facilitators.

This chapter will provide a clear definition of evaluation, including the differences between formative and summative evaluation. It will present some questions that will assist in the design of any evaluation, as well as examine the application of these questions to program evaluation in general and to two specific aspects of program evaluation that are the targets of most evaluative activity: learning outcomes and learning facilitators. A brief discussion of uses of evaluation findings by administrators of adult, community, and continuing education will conclude the chapter.

TOWARD A DEFINITION OF EVALUATION

Over the years, a wide range of definitions of evaluation have been proposed. Some focus on the judgmental aspect of evaluation, the process of determining the extent to which stated objectives are being attained (Tyler, 1949), or whether a discrepancy exists between performance and standards which have been set (Popham, 1969; Provus, 1971). Others focus on the developmental aspect, defining evaluation as the gathering of information for decision making (Cronbach, 1963; Stufflebeam, 1969). In 1981 the Joint Committee on Standards for Educational Evaluation, a group composed of representatives from 12 organizations devoted to educational evaluation, defined *evaluation* as the systematic investigation of the worth or merit of some object. The word *object*, in this definition, can refer to an entire program or to some individual aspect of it, such as learning outcomes, quality of instruction, the marketing function, or recruitment and retention efforts.

In practice, the word *evaluation* means different things to different people, and as Nevo (1983) points out, before one can effectively design an evaluation or discuss the evaluative process it is necessary to clarify, among the parties involved, their perceptions of evaluation in general and of the specific evaluation being proposed.

Formative and Summative Evaluations

Some of the varied definitions of evaluation reflect its diverse roles or functions. Scriven (1967) first proposed the distinction between formative and summative evaluation, and over time, these terms have come to be used to delineate two major categories of evaluation (Nevo, 1983). *Formative evaluation* refers to an ongoing process of gathering data or information about the object of the evaluation (programs, persons, processes, products) which can be used to make needed adjustments. The focus is on improvement and development. Burnham (1995) compares this type of evaluation to "the internal guidance system of a rocket, providing corrective information as it moves toward a target" (p. 5). Formative evaluation answers questions such as: "Is progress being made toward meeting the objectives?" "Are there better approaches which could be used?" "Is intervention, adjustment, or training needed?"

In a *summative evaluation,* the data analysis, and often most of the data gathering, takes place near the end of a program or activity or after it is completed. Accountability is the usual focus; summative evaluations are used to assess the merit or achievement of a program, person, or other object of evaluation usually at the end of a specified period such as a year, a term, or the duration of a learning activity. Summative evaluation answers such questions as: "Were the objectives met?" "Does this program (person, process, product) meet the stated standards?" A summative evaluation, for example, would be used to determine if a program met its goals for the year or if it meets standards for certification, accreditation, or selection for some honor. Figure 7.1 outlines the major differences between formative and summative evaluation.

Ideally, nearly all evaluations in educational settings can and should be used formatively by those being evaluated. While this appears to be a contradiction in terms, it is an important point. Consider these examples: Whether a progam receives accrediatation or fails to be accredited as the result of a summative evaluation, its administrator can and almost surely will choose to use the identification of strengths and weaknesses in the evaluation report to remedy deficiencies and improve the program. If a grant program is continued for additional years because of a positive summative evaluation at the end of the first year, the wise administrator will still use the evaluative information to determine areas of possible improvement; if it is discontinued the information gained will be used to strengthen other programs or future grant proposals. Figure 3.1 in Chapter 3 reflects this philosophy of continuous improvement. Note that the program planning and implementation process is being continually evaluated so that adjustments can be made as the process unfolds (formative evaluation); and the summative evaluation at the end of a particular learning activity or at the end of a program, a year, or some other specified period is viewed not only as an accountability measure but also as an input for future planning.

In addition to the formative and summative functions of evaluations, Nevo (1983) suggests a third major function, the psychological or socio-political function. He notes that evaluation is sometimes used to increase awareness of activities, motivate desired behavior among those being evaluated, or to serve a public relations function.

	Formative Evaluation	Summative Evaluation
Purpose	Proactive, intended to serve decision making Used for improvement and development of an ongoing activity (or program, person, product, etc.)	Retroactive, intended to serve accountability Used for accountability, certification, selection, or continuation
Timing	Done while the action is in progress	Done when the event is nearing completion or after it is over
Central Question	Is maximal progress being made toward meeting the objectives or the standards? If not, where can improvements or modifications be made?	Have the objectives or the standards been met?

Figure 7.1 Formative and summative evaluation: Major differences

SEVEN QUESTIONS TO GUIDE EVALUATION DESIGN

Determining the purpose or function of an evaluation (and there may be several) is a crucial first step, but there are a number of other important considerations. These considerations, reflected as questions, provide a guide to the thought process involved in designing and conducting any evaluation.

1. What is the purpose of the evaluation?

2. Who is the audience for the evaluation?

3. Who should plan and conduct it?

4. What exactly is to be evaluated (objects, aspects, dimensions)?

5. What criteria will be used?

6. What methods will be used?

7. How will the results be analyzed and reported?

Each of these questions will be briefly addressed in the following sections.

What Is the Purpose?

As the demand for accountablilty has accelerated, increasing attention is being given to program evaluation, and certainly the assessment and reporting of results as compared to preset standards is a major purpose of program evaluation. There are, however, many other valuable purposes which can be accomplished through program evaluation. It is also a means of:

- identifying needed changes in procedures or processes
- identifying unmet needs
- gathering data on the differential effectiveness of varied approaches
- determining needed changes in support services, staffing, organizational climate and the like
- examining the appropriateness of program goals and objectives
- gathering data for program promotion

Cranton (1989) states that evaluations of instruction are usually conducted to improve the instruction, make administrative decisions such as program and personnel decisions, and to aid participants in selecting learning activities. Other purposes might include assessing and reporting on performance and identifying appropriate topics for general staff development.

In the area of learners and learning outcomes, the evaluation might be designed to:

- assign grades or certify competence
- determine learner satisfaction with the experience
- determine the impact of the learning experience on learner behavior
- determine the impact of the learners' experience on the wider system (i.e., the workplace or the community)

Grotelueschen (1980) points out that most of the reasons for program evaluation can be categorized on the basis of their time orientation. Evaluations focused on past activities are usually being conducted for the purpose of program justification or accountability; those focused on current efforts seek information for program improvement. Evaluations may also be future-oriented, designed to assist in planning a future educational program. This type of evaluation seeks to determine the worth of potential program goals, alternative means for reaching those goals, and possible consequences of each alternative approach.

As you consider the purpose or purposes of your program evaluation, you will be making decisions which will affect the scope and areas of emphasis included. The annual summative evaluation of an Adult Basic Education (ABE) program conducted by a public institution with state funding will, for example, be sure to include accountability data such as numbers served and program completion rates or increase in proficiency levels. However, you may decide that you want to also do a careful evaluation of recruitment and retention efforts, since the latest census data reveals that you are reaching only a small fraction of the potential target population for this program in your area, or you may want to compare the outcomes resulting from two different instructional approaches. A careful consideration of your purposes at the outset guides your decision making throughout the evaluation process.

Who Is the Audience?

A useful evaluation is one which is designed to meet the needs or requirements of a specific audience. Nevo (1983) distills three important statements related to audiences from the literature on evaluation:

1. An evaluation can have more than one client or audience.

2. Different evaluation audiences might have different evaluation needs.

3. The specific audiences for an evaluation and their evaluation needs have to be clearly identified at the early stages of planning an evaluation. (p. xvii)

Consideration of the audience for the evaluation will affect the types of data that are to be collected and may also affect the way in which the data is analyzed and the results are reported. Typical audiences for program evaluation are funding agencies or parent organizations, the general public, and the individuals involved in the program: administrators, learning facilitators, staff, and program participants. Figure 7.2 provides a more comprehensive range of relevant audiences for program evaluations.

While these same groups will be the usual audiences for the evaluation of learners and learning outcomes, the primary audiences for the results of evaluations of learning facilitators and noninstructional staff are the administrator and the individual involved. A generalized report of group performance or accomplishments may be a useful marketing tool or addition to a program evaluation report, but the results of individual performance appraisals are protected by privacy laws.

Sponsors	Taxpayers
	Funding agencies
	Cooperating agencies
Policy Makers	Federal agencies
	State education departments
	Accrediting bodies
	Central administration
	College or university faculty groups
	Boards of education
Staff	Program planners
	Present and past staff
Clients	Learners
	General public
	Community agencies
	Businesses or other organizations which contract for services
	Agencies with which you have referral
Professional Audiences	Professional associations
	Professional journals
	Other educational agencies

Figure 7.2 A comprehensive range of relevant audiences for program evaluations. This list is an adaptation and expansion of one suggested by Brinkerhoff, Brethower, Hluchyj, & Nowakowski (1983).

Who Should Be on the Evaluation Team?

One of the earliest decisions to be made about an evaluation is whether it is to be directed by an internal or external evaluator. While there may be times when the administrator of an adult, community, or continuing education program chooses to bring in a consultant to examine the entire program or specified parts of it, most routine evaluations are directed by someone within the organization. It is important to designate the evaluation team leader or evaluation director, if the administrator is not assuming this role, in order to avoid the "I thought so-and-so was doing that" syndrome the week before the results are due.

In addition to program administrators and staff, the adult, community, and continuing education literature strongly supports the inclusion of learners in the evaluation process (i.e., Dean 1994; Knowles, 1980; Kowalski, 1988). Kowalski (1988) lists other possible members of the evaluation team: members of a program advisory council; adult, community, or continuing educators from other organizations; persons not actively involved in the program but affected by its outcomes (such as supervisors of the learners); organization employees not involved with the program (such as management staff from other divisions); and former students. The core evaluation team should be small enough to be functional, but large enough to incorporate the program knowledge, technical expertise, and multiple perspectives needed to ensure an appropriate and efficient evaluative process. It is wise, for example, to include from the outset the individual who will assume responsibility for any necessary data processing and analysis. Depending on the magnitude of the evaluation and the type and size of the program, the core team will usually range from four to eight persons.

In the case of faculty or staff evaluations, criteria may be arrived at by an evaluation team, but the evaluations are normally conducted by the adult, community or continuing education administrator or that individual's designee.

What Are the Objects of the Evaluation?

What, exactly, is to be evaluated? The total instructional program? One component of the instructional program? Learner support services? Program management? The extent to which the target population is being reached? The most common objects of evaluation in educational programs are students (or learning outcomes) and faculty (or learning facilitators); however, almost any aspect of a program can be and probably has been evaluated. In the area of community education, for example, in addition to such data as numbers served or classes offered, a variety of other areas may require evaluation, such as extent of cooperative planning or interagency collaboration, use of community resources, or community involvement in program development (Wood & Santellanes, 1977). A sampling of possible objects of evaluation is listed below.

Curriculum-related

- Individual learning activity, such as a course, seminar, workshop, lecture, conference, symposium, community forum
- Group of learning activities related by some common purpose or topic, such as a certificate program, a degree program, or a lecture series
  Examples: GED preparation program, real estate recertification program, legal assistant preparation program, community action project

- Need and interest assessment processes
- Self-instructional materials
- Staffing, resources, and use of a learning resource center
- Comparative effectiveness of different instructional approaches

Management-related

- Management system
- Internal communications
- Records management
- Budget management
- Staff development program
- Recruitment and retention of students
- Recruitment and retention of staff
- Marketing and promotion

Once the object or objects of the evaluation are clearly identified, the next step is to decide on the aspects or dimensions of the object that will be examined. Stufflebeam's (1983) model of program evaluation, for example, recommends examination of four areas of a program:

1. *Context*: type of organization, method of funding, program staffing patterns, organizational climate

2. *Input*: resources available to and used by the program in meeting its goals, such as personnel, funding level, volunteers

3. *Process*: how well the program was implemented

4. *Product*: qualitative and quantitative program outcomes

What Criteria Will Be Used?

The most common criteria for evaluation are those stated in program goals and objectives. This fact underlines the importance of developing clear, measurable objectives wherever it is feasible to do so. While some argue that evaluation criteria should emerge directly from the program objectives, others caution that objectives set at the beginning of a program do not necessarily provide adequate criteria for evaluation. It may be that the objectives were poorly constructed initially or that important areas of emphasis were omitted; that circumstances or needs changed dramatically during the period covered by the evaluation, necessitating program changes; or that new leadership has resulted in new program emphases. In addition, as stated in Chapter 3, important affective objectives may be omitted if they are difficult to state in measurable form. Brinkerhoff et al. (1983) recommend that, in addition to achievement of intended outcomes, the criteria include responsiveness to needs, ideals, and values; optimal use of available resources and opportunities; and adherence to effective practice.

Comprehensive program evaluation usually includes such criteria from the program objectives as numbers served, stated in terms of a numerical goal or a percentage increase, numbers of learning activites offered, and learning outcomes. Criteria within the area of learner outcomes might include such things as an acceptable range of difference in pretest/posttest results or other quantifiable achievements. One criterion which is almost universal in the evaluation of learning facilitators is a specified level of achievement on some measure of performance in which the learners are the evaluators.

What Methods Will Be Used?

Notice that the word *methods* is plural. One area of agreement among educational evaluators is that the use of multiple methods greatly improves the accuracy of an evaluation. The quality of a particular learning activity, for example, can be measured by a subjective participant rating sheet, an attitude inventory, an objective test, dropout rate, intent to enroll in future courses, or a variety of other means. The evaluation team chooses the methods on the basis of appropriateness and feasibility, taking into consideration the evaluation questions to be answered and the audience to which the results are to be presented as well as the time, money, and human resources available for data collection and analysis.

Evaluation processes in adult, community, and continuing education often include the collection of both *quantitative* and *qualitative* data. *Quantitative* procedures, such as tests or rating sheets, produce results in terms of numbers that can be summarized or compared, making them very compatible with measurable behavioral objectives. In contrast, *qualitative* procedures produce narrative information, which is more difficult to summarize. Qualitative procedures are used to provide a broader perspective of the object of the evaluation (Brinkerhoff et al., 1983; Merriam & Simpson, 1995; Steele, 1990) and to obtain evaluative data on the affective outcomes, the attitudes and perceptions that are so important but sometimes difficult to assess (Patton, 1987, 1990). Examples of qualitative procedures include case studies, collection of open-ended comments, interviews, observations, and records analysis. The same data collection instrument may be designed to collect both qualitative and quantitative information. For example, a faculty or staff evaluation instrument might include a number of items to be rated on a scale of 1–5 as well as an open-ended question or comment section. Several commonly used qualitative and quantitative procedures and instruments are listed in Figure 7.3.

The adult, community, or continuing education administrator's role in determining learning outcomes at the course or activity level (micro level), like the role in the determination of program content at this level, is less active. Certain procedures may be mandated, such as periodic testing of students in remedial adult programs to assess progress in attainment of basic skills which will be reported as a part of the comprehensive program evaluation. Standard evaluation forms might be used at the conclusion of each course or activity as a matter of policy or in response to an institutional requirement. In some cases, such as vocational courses using government funding, tracking of students and analysis of their success in getting and holding a job is a mandatory part of the evaluation. Often, however, the learning facilitator is entirely responsible for the development and administration of the evaluation of learning outcomes at the course or activity level. The methods used vary widely, depending on the content of the learning activity and whether it is a credit or noncredit offering.

Common methods used in the evaluation of learning facilitators include performance checklists or other reports of structured observations and analysis of measures of learner satisfaction such as attitude scales. In credit courses or courses designed to prepare students for a credentialing examination, tracking of student achievement by the learning facilitator may be used as part of the learning facilitator's evaluation. In continuing education, for example, learner success rates on a real estate licensing examination or an accounting recertification examination could be part of a learning facilitator's evaluation.

How Will the Results Be Reported?

The usefulness of an evaluation depends largely on the degree to which the intended audiences become aware of the findings, accept them, and recognize the implications for action. Cronbach (1982) points out

Qualitative procedures

   Case studies
   Interviews
   Simulations
   Records analysis
   Interaction analysis
   Logs
   Systems analysis
   Analysis of physical evidence

Quantitative procedures

   Knowledge tests
   Opinion surveys
   Performance checklists
   Behavior checklists
   Self-rating scales
   Q-sorts
   Delphi technique
   Surveys

Figure 7.3 Some qualitative and quantitative evaluation procedures

that the reporting task of an evaluator is a complex one because multiple audiences are involved. The audiences may be very diverse in terms of perspectives, levels of knowledge, or familiarity with terms commonly used in educational evaluation. In addition, as discussed earlier in this chapter, an evaluation often has multiple purposes. The multiple audiences and multiple purposes usually result in a variety of ways of reporting evaluation results, some formal and some informal (Morris, Fitz-Gibbon, & Freeman, 1987).

Examples of formal reports include a written report for a funding agency or accrediting agency, an oral presentation to a school board, an advisory board, a college or university committee, a faculty group, or an administrator. Informal reports might take the form of a newsletter article, press release, memo, announcement, or brief oral report.

Guidelines for Evaluation Reports

Although certainly not comprehensive, the following guidelines will help you avoid some of the problems that frequently interfere with the communication of evaluaton results to the intended audiences.

Use Appropriate Language. A funding agency or accrediting agency will understand the "educationese" related to evaluation. A community group or advisory committee will understand and respond better to a translation into more common terminology.

Use Visuals. Graphs and charts can help you communicate your results quickly and clearly.

Cover all the Bases. In a formal report, make sure you have addressed all the areas required or requested. When preparing informal communications, consider what your audience will be most interested in as well as what you want to make sure they know.

Include Implications and Recommendations for Action. The effective administrator is always seeking ways to improve program and process.

USING THE EVALUATION RESULTS

Sork (1991) points out that adherence to the basic tenets of program planning does not guarantee participation; participation does not guarantee success. If your program is a normal one, the evaluation will reveal some successes and some failures. Both can yield useful information. In the process of analyzing and interpreting the evaluation results, the evaluation team gains valuable insights on the strengths and weaknesses of your program as well as possible implications for action or areas for further investigation. Make sure these insights are not lost. Ask your evaluation team to prepare a written list of recommendations, and then discuss the list in order to gain the maximum benefit from the team's experience.

The next step is to develop an action plan which addresses the recommendations of the evaluation team. Ideally, some of the members of the evaluation team or some of the individuals who served as liaisons with an outside team will be a part of this process. While it is understandable that there is a tendency to focus on the weaknesses and the ways in which they might be corrected, it is important that the action plan also address ways to continue or improve effectiveness in other areas.

The timing of the action planning session can have a major impact on the commitment it produces and the success of its implementation. If it takes place shortly after the results are reported, the immediacy and familiarity can contribute to more productive brainstorming. One caution: There may be individuals who need to be involved in the action planning session but feel threatened by the evaluation results. The administrator may want to meet privately with these individuals to assist them in dealing with the emotions involved before the action planning session takes place.

SUMMARY

After providing an overview of evaluation and clarifying the differences between formative and summative evaluation, this chapter presents seven questions to guide evaluation design. These questions address (1) the purpose of the evaluation, (2) the audience for which the evaluation is being completed, (3) the composition of the evaluation team, (4) object(s) of the evaluation, (5) criteria to be used, (6) methods to be used, and (7) the way in which the results are to be analyzed and reported. Each question is discussed in turn. The final section of the chapter recommends a process for ensuring that the results of the evaluation are used.

In each and every administrative function and task, there are legal and ethical considerations. The next chapter examines some of these concerns confronting the adult, community, and continuing education administrator.

CHAPTER 8

Legal and Ethical Considerations

Problems facing administrators in adult, community, and continuing education are really opportunities since so much of our business involves change. We conduct needs assessments to determine program priorities, convert these priorities into learning formats such as courses or workshops, market our programs with the aim of responding to the identified needs of various clientele, and evaluate the quality of our programmatic and instructional efforts. Behind all of these efforts are certain legal and ethical obligations we have to our organization, our customers, our profession, and most importantly, to ourselves.

In times past, when life seemed simple and our work was relatively free from federal, state, and provincial regulations, it may have been possible to leave the legal "stuff" to the attorneys or legal advisors. A verbal agreement, handshake, or nod of the head was all that was necessary to close a deal. Today, this is no longer possible. There are all sorts of legal requirements that must be handled by a skilled administrator of adult, community, and continuing education. These range from personnel matters such as affirmative action and equal employment opportunity practices to contractual arrangements with conference facilities and food service operations. In addition, there are certain ethical obligations associated with the business of adult, community, and continuing education that require forethought and reflection.

The purpose of this chapter is to look at some of the legal issues and ethical obligations facing administrators in adult, community, and continuing education. We start by discussing affirmative action and equal employment opportunity guidelines related to hiring practices for personnel. Next, discussion shifts to an overview of the Americans with Disabilities Act of 1990 and some of the implications associated with the law. We continue our discussion of legal aspects by focusing attention on contractual agreements with facilities, paid staff, and volunteers. Finally, we look at the business of ethics and certain ethical dilemmas confronting administrators in adult, community, and continuing education with the aim of improving practice.

ORIGINS OF AFFIRMATIVE ACTION AND EQUAL EMPLOYMENT OPPORTUNITIES

Beginning in the early sixties, the U.S. federal government became actively involved in attempting to ensure the fair and equitable treatment of all employees in the public and private sectors of organizational life (Lewis, Lewis, & Ponterotto, 1990; Uris, 1988). Affirmative action, as it is popularly known was initiated by the John F. Kennedy administration and later championed by Lyndon Johnson to help eliminate job discrimination in the areas of hiring, promotion, training opportunities, compensation practices, employee benefits, and firing (Bills & Hall, 1994). As the employment playing field grew less balanced, Johnson signed an executive order in 1965 requiring all federal contractors to develop and implement an affirmative action program. Basically, the program required any federal contractor receiving government funds of more than $10,000 to implement an affirmative action program that forced contractors to consider whites, minorities, and women equally (Brown, 1995).

Attempts to ensure equality did not end with Johnson's efforts; in 1969, Richard Nixon supported equal employment opportunities in federal departments and agencies through the Civil Service Commission. The physically handicapped received attention from the Gerald Ford administration in 1976. Through Jimmy Carter the Committee on Equal Opportunity was implemented, which coordinated federal equal opportunity programs (Brown, 1995).

The 1980s ushered a more passive attempt at equal opportunity with Ronald Reagan's administration encouraging, rather than mandating, the use of federal funds to support minority businesses. The Bush administration continued a reduced federal role in equal rights by implementing a policy outlawing scholarships available to minority students. Now, as part of Clinton's administration, affirmative action has again entered center stage as politicians and journalists argue over the pros and cons of affirmative action. Ironically, a political movement intended to correct some long-standing social wrongs is currently being questioned by many Americans along the political spectrum with the issue of "fairness" hovering somewhere in the middle (Brown, 1995; Coomes, 1994).

Regardless of the current debate over affirmative action and equal employment opportunities, most administrators in adult, community, and continuing education must be at least familiar with federal guidelines since many programs receive external funding for programming and financial aid. For example, adult literacy programs for disadvantaged adults are often federally funded as are selected jobs programs. The same is true for many cultural programs funded through the National Endowment for the Arts and the National Endowment for the Humanities. Also, many adult students receive financial aid to either continue, finish, or update their education.

HIGHLIGHTS OF AFFIRMATIVE ACTION AND EQUAL EMPLOYMENT OPPORTUNITY GUIDELINES

Title VII of the Civil Rights Act of 1964 serves as the core legislation for antidiscrimination laws pertaining to affirmative action and equal employment opportunities. The law prohibits discrimination on the basis of race, color, religion, sex, or nationality and covers the following: employers engaged in an industry affecting interstate commerce who have at least 15 full-time employees in 20 or more weeks of the existing calender year; labor organizations that maintain a hiring hall or have at least 15 members; employment agencies; state and local governments; certain federal government units; and, educational institutions. There are some exempt agencies including certain federal government units, Indian tribes, religious and government organizations, and bona fide private membership clubs. Enforcement of affirmative action is provided by the Equal Employment Opportunity Commission (EEOC) (Uris, 1988). In order to employ personnel, affected agencies are required to prepare an affirmative action plan that shows compliance with the Guidelines on Affirmative Action issued by the EEOC. These plans are usually updated annually to reflect current guideline changes, new laws, or administrative and agency experience.

Basically, an affirmative action plan is a comprehensive tool designed to help the agency demonstrate how EEOC guidelines are met. The plan identifies who has primary responsibility for the affirmative action program, explicates fair employment goals and timetables for completion, describes the advertising, recruiting, and hiring procedures followed by the agency, lists the policies and procedures for handling employee complaints such as sexual harassment, and delineates ongoing means of evaluating compliance with the law. Depending on the complexity of the adult, community, and continuing education agency, affirmative action and equal employment opportunity guidelines are handled by the personnel office under the direction of a supervising administrator.

Compliance Commitments: An Overview

In addition to the Civil Rights Act of 1964, Title VII, there are several other federal laws and regulations related to equal employment opportunity. Prominent among these are the following:

1. The Executive Order No. 11246, which was issued by President Johnson in 1965 to prohibit race discrimination by federal contractors and to require them to undertake affirmative action to employ and promote minorities. The order was amended in 1967 to encompass women as well as minorities.

2. The Rehabilitation Act of 1973, which governs the rights of disabled individuals. Section 503 of the Act requires federal government contractors to undertake affirmative action to ensure that employment opportunities are provided to persons with disabilities. Section 504 prohibits discrimination in any program or activity receiving federal assistance.

3. The Vietnam Era Veterans Readjustment Assistance Act of 1974, which requires government contractors and subcontractors to take affirmative action with respect to certain classes of veterans. Contractors are required to prepare written affirmative action plans. The law also provides reemployment rights for individuals who leave their jobs to serve in the armed forces.

4. The 1978 Amendments to the Civil Rights Act of 1964, which bans pregnancy discrimination.

5. Title IX of the Education Amendments of 1972, which prohibits discrimination based on sex.

6. The Equal Pay Act of 1963, which prohibits discrimination based on sex in the payment of wages.

7. The Age Discrimination in Employment Act of 1967 and subsequent amendments in 1978, which prohibit discrimination against individuals above the age of 40.

8. Civil Rights Act of 1991 (CRA) which reverses eight Supreme Court rulings that narrowed the scope and effectiveness of federal employment discrimination laws. Also, it strengthens the protection of discrimination laws and expands their remedies. The purpose of the CRA is to provide remedies for intentional discrimination and unlawful harassment in the workplace (Lewis, Lewis & Ponterotto, 1990 Vialpando, 1994).

Pitfalls to Avoid in Application Blanks and Interviews

There are some definite pitfalls associated with employment applications and the interview process regarding an applicant's race, color, religion, or natural origin. Special care should be taken to avoid asking unlawful questions or straying into areas of inquiry that are touchy. Uris (1988) provides a brief summary of questions to avoid in the hiring process:

- Original name of an applicant whose name had been legally changed.
- Birthplace of applicant, applicant's parents, spouse or other relatives.
- Requirements that applicant submit birth certificate, naturalization, or baptismal record.
- Inquiry into an applicant's religious denomination, religious affiliations, church, parish, pastor, or religious holidays observed.
- Requirement that an applicant affix a photograph to his or her employment form after interview.
- Inquiry into whether an applicant's parents or spouse are naturalized or native-born citizens; the date when any of the above acquired citizenship.
- Questions about marital status, number of children, or childbearing plans.
- Questions about child-care arrangements.
- Inquiry into language commonly used by applicant.
- Inquiry into how applicant acquired the ability to read, write, or speak a foreign language.
- Requirement that an applicant list all clubs, societies, and lodges to which he or she belongs.
- Inquiry into an applicant's general military experience.

Even though there is a good deal of debate underway regarding affirmative action and equal employment opportunities which may lead to some adjustments in the law, skilled administrators of adult, community, and continuing education will need to keep abreast of any changes. This section provided a brief overview of the law and some key points to think about when engaging in hiring practices. Another area of concern is the Americans with Disabilities Act which is described below.

THE AMERICANS WITH DISABILITIES ACT: AN OVERVIEW

Established by the U.S. Congress and signed into law by George Bush on July 25, 1990, the Americans with Disabilities Act (ADA) extends the mandate for nondiscrimination on the basis of disability to the private sector and the nonfederal public sector including state and local government. According to Jarrow (1993) "the ADA is generally considered to be the most sweeping piece of civil rights legislation passed in more than twenty-five years" (p. 15). It extends Section 504 of the Rehabilitation Act of 1973 by imposing a responsibility on postsecondary institutions not to discriminate on the basis of disability and to provide individuals with meaningful access. As far as the impact on adult, community, and continuing education is concerned, ADA affects employment, academic programs, and facility construction (Bausch, 1994; Bills & Hall, 1994).

The ADA provides that "no covered entity shall discriminate against a qualified individual with a disability because of the disability of such individual in regard to job application procedures, the hiring, advancement, or discharge of employees, employee compensation, job training, and other terms, conditions, and privileges of employment" (42 U.S.C. § 12112 [a]). It guarantees equal opportunity for individuals with disabilities in employment, public accommodations, transportation, state and local government services, and telecommunications (Kearney, 1992).

Who is considered disabled? The EEOC defines a disabled person as one who has a physical or mental condition that substantially impairs a major life activity such as walking, breathing, seeing, or the ability to work, or one who has a history of impairment such as a chronic condition that has lasted more than 6 months, or is regarded by others as having such an impairment (ADA Compliance Guide, 1990). In practical terms, the ADA protects any qualified individual with a disability who can perform the essential functions of a job. The act uses "essential functions" to mean those duties described on a written job description as evidence of the job's essential functions. Thus, administrators must define the essential qualifications of a job in the position description (Bills & Hall, 1994). The ADA does exclude certain disabilities from its definition including "homosexuality, bisexuality, . . . transvestism, transsexualism, pedophilia, exhibitionism, voyeurism, gender identity, kleptomania, and pyromania" (42 U.S.C. § 12211 [a] and [b]). In addition, current illegal drug users are excluded from the ADA.

The ADA is divided into four sections known as titles which address different aspects of the law. Title I provides important employment definitions regarding jobs held by a person with a disability and designates the regulatory body of Title I as the Equal Employment Opportunity Commission (EEOC). Title II focuses on reasonable accommodations for a disabled person with respect to public services and transportation. The regulatory body for Title II is the Department of Transportation. Title III is regulated by the Justice Department and prohibits privately owned and operated businesses from denying goods, programs, and services to disabled persons. Places like museums, libraries, theaters, restaurants, hotels, and professional buildings must accommodate patrons with a disability through physical accessibility, auxiliary aids, or the like. Title IV is targeted at federally regulated telecommunications, such as telephone companies, cable systems, and public broadcast. The law requires telephone companies to provide appropriate equipment for the hearing- and speech-impaired and closed-captioning for hearing-impaired viewers of public service messages. The regulatory agency for Title IV is the Federal Communications Commission (Kearney, 1992).

Meaningful Access and Reasonable Accommodations

The Americans with Disabilities Act of 1990 requires institutions to provide meaningful access and reasonable accommodations for disabled persons. What this means is that a qualified disabled person must be treated the same as a qualified nondisabled person in the work or programmatic setting. Thus, academic institutions including programs in adult, community, and continuing education "cannot refuse to provide deaf students with interpreter services, deny auxiliary aids to students in nondegree programs, fail to accommodate mobility-impaired students in its business education laboratory, refuse to make a new swimming pool accessible to mobility-impaired students, or fail to give disabled individuals transportation services that are equal to or as effective as those offered to nondisabled persons" (Heyward, 1993, p. 19).

One of the problems in operationalizing the obligations academic institutions have in providing reasonable accommodations to disabled persons is that the law is rather nebulous in defining the term. According to Kearney (1992), this was purposeful and meant to promote voluntary cooperation among institutions in complying with the law. However, there are 19 key factors dealing with physical accommodations that administrators can use in auditing facilities and structural designs in meeting the ADA code. The factors cover all issues identified by people with disabilities as critical to their successful use of environments as employees, guests, patrons, and citizens (Kearney, 1992). The factors are used as a guide for the design and modification of new or existing space; the specific location, needs of the institution and disabled person(s) will dictate how the factors are actually addressed.

Kearney (1992) describes the key factors below:

1. **Accessibility:** Mobility within a space, manipulation of objects and equipment within a space, and ease of participation in activities throughout should be ensured.

2. **Adaptability:** Flexible furnishings, equipment and fixtures should allow reasonable accommodation, no matter what the disability.

3. **Comfort:** Design should fit equipment to people, not people to equipment.

4. **Communication:** Communication should be enhanced with quiet rooms and modes of communication that fit the strengths of the person.

5. **Density:** A feeling of spaciousness and high visibility are important.

6. **Division of Space:** Space should be divided to integrate people around the use of shared equipment. The status of a location for a disabled person is the degree to which access is enhanced.

7. **Equipment:** Technology should be provided to enhance capability without compromising disability (controls, keyboards, on computer hardware and software). Adaptive and assistive devices increase the opportunity to be independent.

8. **Finishes:** All surfaces should be easily maintained, with either smooth wall coverings and/or laminated surfaces.

9. **Image:** Coordination of color and furnishings with existing furnishings enhances image and comfort.

10. **Lighting:** Individual task lighting should be provided as needed to prevent fatigue. Full spectrum total room lighting is easiest on one's eyes. Glare control is essential.

11. **Maintenance:** Minimum maintenance should be required, thereby reducing attention to the needs of the disabled.

12. **Noise:** Noise should be minimized as it is a fatigue factor that lowers everyone's resistance to stress.

14. **Passages:** Mapping a building properly is essential for ease of access.

15. **Safety:** Safety is a primary concern for everyone, disabled or not.

16. **Signage:** Signage should clearly guide the newest person to any area of the building. Luminescence and lettering are critical.

17. **Storage:** Storage areas should be accessible and uncluttered to allow independent access to supplies.

18. **Temperature/Air Quality:** If possible, it is preferable to zone individual needs.

19. **Windows:** Natural light is the best, psychologically.

INTERVIEWING EMPLOYEES/APPLICANTS: SOME QUESTIONS THAT CAN BE ASKED AND SOME THAT CANNOT

Interviewing potential employees is a vital function in all organizations including adult, community, and continuing education. Interviews help employers assess the strengths of potential employees and determine optimum fit for the organization. Just as with affirmative action and equal employment opportunity practices, there are some appropriate and inappropriate questions to ask during an interview associated with ADA. Here are some appropriate commonly asked questions (Kearney, 1992):

1. What is your attendance record at school or your present job?

2. Do you have a license or certificate to _____?
   (Fill in blank with license or certificate necessary to teach, drive, etc.)

3. Where did you go to school and why?

4. What organization are you affiliated with now, or have been affiliated with in the past, as a volunteer which shows your experience or qualifications for the position for which you have applied?

5. Who referred you here?

6. What are your personal and professional goals?

7. State the names, addresses, and telephone numbers of your previous employers, why you accepted the job, and why you left the job.

8. Do you have the ability to perform the job functions?

9. On what basis do you believe you are qualified for the position(s) for which you have applied?

10. What work experience(s) have you had that make you qualified for the position(s) for which you have applied?

11. What are your employment strengths and weaknesses as related to this job?

12. Are you willing to accept employment on condition that you pass a job-related physical examination?

While there are some legitimate questions that can and should be asked as part of the interview process, there are some definite no-nos. Here are some questions to avoid (Kearney, 1992):

1. Do you have a physical or mental handicap or disability?

2. How did you become disabled?

3. Would you need special or expensive accommodations to do the job for which you have applied?

4. Do you have epilepsy, multiple sclerosis, etc.?

5. What medication, if any, do you take on a regular basis?

6. Are there any restrictions on your driver's license?

7. Do you commonly become tired at work in the afternoon?

8. Are you often too tired to get to work on time in the morning?

9. Can you travel independently?

10. Do any of your children, your spouse, or others in your family have physical or mental handicaps?

11. Is your diet restricted for any reason?

Complaints or Disputes

Avoiding complaints or disputes associated with employment practices is certainly the best solution. The ideal way to avoid them is to have a well-written compliance plan that communicates clearly to all parties in the adult, community, and continuing education organization what is reasonable and acceptable conduct. In the event that a complaint or dispute arises, it is probably best to try and deal with the situation in a direct, professional manner. Consulting legal advisors to the organization, those responsible for certifying the compliance plan, and the appropriate federal agency are certainly good ways of protecting everyone's rights and responsibilities.

USING CONTRACTS AND PUTTING THINGS IN WRITING

It probably goes without saying, but we'll say it anyway. The keys to successfully administering adult, community, and continuing education programs can be reduced to four basic rules: put everything in writing, be flexible, plan thoroughly, and expect the unexpected (Winter, 1994). There are many examples of best laid plans going for nought. If we make a mistake once in a while, that's okay. But if mistakes are regular occurrences, then something is wrong and should be corrected. Very often, the root of those "regular" mistakes can be traced to two things: (1) avoiding the use of contracts, and (2) not putting things in writing. This section looks at some ways of eliminating those "regular" mistakes by exploring the use of contracts and putting things in writing.

Types and Uses of Contracts

Contracts are commonly used in nearly every place we look these days. They are used in the business world to specify an arrangement for goods and services at a fixed price. In the entertainment and sports fields, they are used to dramatize the signing of a noted celebrity or sports figure. In adult, community, and continuing education, contracts are often used to specify arrangements with conference or hotel facilities, food service operations, exhibitors, and other auxiliary enterprises. Contracts may also be used with full-time instructors, administrators, and support staff, and sometimes they are used to list duties of volunteer tutors, part-time faculty, and docents. Certainly, the idea of having a record or letter of agreement makes good business sense. But sometimes, preparing a contract may be overlooked. Skilled administrators of adult, community, and continuing education have learned the value of using contracts, often the hard way. They may have relied on a verbal commitment or their short-term memory only to discover someone not following through or changing the agreement at the last minute.

Contracts take a number of forms in adult, community, and continuing education just as they do in other organizations. A job description for a full-time instructor or clerical staff member is one common example and is similar to a contract. A letter of agreement with a consulting firm doing marketing is another contract form. Yet another example is a memorandum written to a client detailing certain responsibilities, activity timeline, and performance specifications. In all of these examples, it is critical to have some record of agreement that specifies what is to happen, when it is to happen, where it is to happen, who it will happen to, along with some sense of how well the arrangement is carried out. In many respects, having a written record protects all parties involved, from clients to the adult, community, and continuing education organization itself. Avoiding or forgetting to put something in writing may have deleterious effects and account for those regular mistakes noted above.

Information to Include in a Contract

The information to include in a contract is related to its purpose. If, for example, the contract is for a faculty member, a job description may be most appropriate. Essential information might include the basic qualifications and experience for the job such as a graduate degree in a particular discipline and so many years teaching in adult education. In addition, the specific duties are then listed by categories such as teaching, research, and service. Finally, any negotiated adjustments to the assignment might be noted on the form along with space for the employee's signature, the program chair, director or dean, and the academic vice president.

If the contract is for a conference at a hotel or convention center, a more elaborate and detailed form might be used. Typically, the following information is included in this kind of contract (Winter, 1994):

- Prices and rates for sleeping rooms, meeting rooms, and exhibit space
- Labor charges for room setups, electricians, and so forth
- Mutual expectations of the conference and the facility regarding performance
- Deadlines, including release dates for meeting room and sleeping room blocks
- Prices and rates for food services including meal functions, breaks, and catered events
- Rental rates for audiovisual equipment such as overhead projectors, television monitors, and videotape recorders
- Remedies for breach of contract or default on either side
- Mechanisms to avoid future disputes
- A cancellation clause spelling out any financial penalties, forms of restitution, and legal arrangements should litigation occur

In addition to a formal contract, a letter of agreement highlighting key points is a good thing to do. Usually, this letter is prepared by the agent responsible for the hotel property or convention center and is sent to the person in charge of the upcoming event. Remember, as important as it is to put everything in writing, it is equally important to read the contract and accompanying letter thoroughly before signing. At this point, it may make sense to involve key staff and the legal office in reviewing the materials. Once signed, the contract becomes binding and it is often expensive to request any changes to the agreement; if there are any changes they usually are at the sponsoring agency's expense.

Improving Communication by Spelling Out Expectations

There are a number of advantages for using contracts and spelling out expectations. Chief among them is improved communication. Having a clear sense of what one is doing and the level of expectation helps ensure some degree of accountability among all parties. This is especially true for paid staff who should be evaluated on a periodic basis. But don't forget the volunteers or docents. Having a job description or letter of agreement is as helpful for the volunteer as it is for the paid employee since it gives the person a tool for understanding expected duties and responsibilities. When this written arrangement occurs, paid staff are better able to manage volunteers and improve communication for the entire organization. Just because an adult, community, or continuing education organization relies heavily on volunteers is no excuse for avoiding job descriptions or contractual agreements. In fact, it may be all the more important.

ETHICS IN ADULT, COMMUNITY, AND CONTINUING EDUCATION

Ethics and codes of ethics play a major role in most professions, especially in the service areas where others are affected. Some of these professions include medicine, law, counseling, social work, and securities. In adult, community, and continuing education there is no formally established code of ethics partly because of the diversity of organizations providing services to adults and the multiple roles played by practitioners in working with adults (Sisco, 1988). Certainly, ethics play an important role in adult, community, and continuing education, but the debate over how to best ensure ethical practice continues.

Recently, a plethora of authors have written about ethics and the need for a code of ethics in adult, community, and continuing education (Brockett, 1988a, 1990; Carlson, 1988; Connelly & Light, 1991; Cunningham, 1992; Freeman, Shaeffer, & Whitson, 1993; Griffith, 1991; McDonald & Wood, Jr., 1993; Rose, 1993; Sisco, 1988; Sork & Welock, 1992; Walker, 1993; Zinn, 1993). Although these authors advocate particular positions on the issue, actual research focusing on ethics and a code of ethics in adult, community, and continuing education is rather sparse. In fact, McDonald and Wood, Jr., (1993) contend that "empirical research on ethics in adult education is almost nonexistent in the professional literature" (p. 243). The concerned reader might ask why is this the case? Rose (1993) explains that "Much of the debate within the literature deals with the question of whether or not a code of ethics is the best way to address ethical problems and dilemmas. Such a focus, while important, narrows the lens through which we analyze and understand the ethical and moral questions relating to adult education. Much of this debate goes on despite the paucity of research into the ethical traditions that make up the pluralistic totality of adult education" (p. 5).

Clearly, ethics and associated dilemmas do exist in adult, community, and continuing education since so much of our work involves the human enterprise. In fact, nearly every decision we make has an ethical component to it. Even though the prospect of a universally accepted code of ethics may be beyond our reach, some discussion of the meaning of ethics and associated dilemmas in adult, community, and continuing education seems appropriate. We will begin our discussion with an overview of what ethics mean.

The Meaning of Ethics

The study of ethics has occupied human beings since antiquity. The Greek philosopher Aristotle contended that people engage in ethical questioning in order to conduct their lives "rightly" and "reasonably." He believed that ethics had a practical quality leading to a fuller and richer life. The idea of a fuller life so consumed Socrates that his life was ended because of high ideals. To Socrates, it was far more important to die than to recant his beliefs about human beings and their relationship to society; that's taking an ethical stance!

According to Brockett (1988b), ethics consist of at least two major aspects. First, it is a branch of philosophy that focuses upon moral questions. In addition, ethics refer to a set of beliefs that guide human action and interaction. To this we might add that ethics "is the process of taking one's understanding of "good" or "right" behavior and applying it to the decisions one makes in everyday life. Beliefs and values are inextricably woven into one's ethical standards. Acting ethically, or making an ethical decision, is the operationalization of what one considers to be the correct, right, or best way to behave" (Merriam, 1988, p. 146).

The relationship between ethics and values is sometimes misunderstood. Values are beliefs that guide our attitudes and actions. Some values are ethical and some are ethically neutral because they do not relate to moral conduct or obligations. According to Walker (1993), ethically neutral values "concern things that are personally important such as financial security, professional success, personal freedom, or social relationships" (p. 13). Walker explains that "Individuals develop personal value systems that guide their behavior. Such a value system is not the same as a code of ethics, because there is no standard of evaluation other than personal opinion" (p. 13). Brockett (1988b) contends that values become particularly important in ethical situations where there is a need to choose among two or more possible courses of action. He believes that values become internalized at several different levels ranging from initial acceptance to personal commitment. In Brockett's mind, "These levels of internalizations are most important since they define the limits of acceptable behavior in a given situation" (p. 11).

The Roots of Ethical Dilemmas

Ethical dilemmas emanate from a variety of situations and often involve making one or more choices that may result in a breach of acceptable behavior. Alternatively, ethical dilemmas occur when taking action is based on sacrificing one moral conviction for another (Zinn, 1993).

In many respects, ethical dilemmas are situationally based and may lead to a "means justifying the ends" rationalization. Consider the following. You are an administrator of an outreach program in continuing higher education. A major part of your job is increasing the number of student registrations in the various degree programs offered by the institution. You know that there is a 12 credit-hour limit imposed by the graduate school which means hours taken beyond the limit will not count on graduate degree programs unless a person is formally admitted to study. You also know that unless there is a steady increase in registrations, your job may be on the line. You decide that it is more important to keep registrations high and cash profits flowing than informing participants of the 12-hour rule and warning of lost credits if they continue to take courses unless admitted to a degree program.

Imagine you are a counselor in an adult literacy program. You know that some of the clients are accepting cash payments for seasonal work while they are receiving financial aid. Many of these clients are single parents with little or no discretionary income. If you report these "transgressions" to the authorities, you will likely harm the children more than the parent since he/she may face legal charges, lose income, and be taken from the children. You rationalize that it is probably better to look the other way and do nothing than to turn the offenders in.

Consider another situation. Suppose you are aware of poor student evaluations of a particular individual who has political ties to the local school district. You need this person's support because many aspiring teachers in the College of Education do their student teaching in the district. You rationalize that it is probably better to overlook poor student evaluations than potentially harm the entire student teaching program that is needed for certification.

Recognizing Ethical Dilemmas

Ethical dilemmas are inherent in most aspects of adult, community, and continuing education and recognizing them is important to good practice. For example, they are embedded in conflicts of interest, unfair competition, teaching evaluations, truth in advertising, power differentials between teachers and students and supervisors and employees, perceived value of time and money spent, breach of confidentiality, or failure to give proper credit for something. Zinn (1993) offers a number of questions you might ask yourself to see if an ethical dilemma exists:

1. When I (or others) talk about this matter, do we use key words or phrases such as "right or wrong," "black or white," "fair or unfair," "bottom line," "should," "appropriate," "ethical," "conflict," or "values"?

2. Is there any question of legality? Violation of professional standards or codes of ethics?

3. Will there be potential harm to anyone as a result of my decision/action, or of my failure to act?

4. Am I concerned about my decision being equally fair to all parties?

5. Do I feel a conflict between my personal values and professional interests (e.g., institutional goals or client needs)?

6. Is there any controversy or strong opposition regarding this decision? Will it be divisive in some way?

7. Will I be hesitant to reveal my decision about this matter to others? Would I take the same action in a "clean, well-lit room"?

8. Do I have a gut feeling that something is not quite "right" about this?

9. Is this a decision that nobody else wants to make?

If you answered yes to several of these questions, you are probably facing an ethical dilemma (Zinn, 1993, p. 8).

Common Ethical Dilemmas in Adult, Community, and Continuing Education

There is high probability that you will face any number of ethical dilemmas in your role as an administrator of adult, community, and continuing education. As the saying goes, "It comes with the turf!" Yet, articulating some of these common dilemmas may be helpful in thinking through your response to each dilemma. Singarella and Sork (1983) highlight a number of the more enduring dilemmas in adult education— especially as they pertain to program planning—by posing a series of fundamental questions that may impact our practice:

1. Should adult educators always respond to client "felt" needs?

2. Should adult educators undertake or prescribe therapeutic learning transactions in cases where clients may not recognize that a learning need exists?

3. Should adult educators ever abandon the goal of fostering self-directed learning in order to achieve a specific learning outcome?

4. Should adult educators aspire to change social systems through their influence on changing individuals?

5. Should adult educators continue to emphasize individual learning deficiencies as a basis for programs?

6. Should adult educators ever knowingly plan programs in which learners will be compelled to participate?

7. Should information collected as part of a needs assessment ever be released to anyone outside the learning transaction?

8. To what extent should adult educators limit claims regarding efficacy of their programs?

9. Should adult educators conceal objectives of their programs from potential participants?

10. Should adult educators use funds collected from one group to finance programs for a different client group?

11. Should adult educators withhold the results of program evaluations?

There are many other ethical questions that could be posed in the context of adult, community, and continuing education; recognizing them is one thing, doing something about them is another.

Making Ethical Decisions

There is probably nothing more agonizing than making decisions that involve people, especially those we like. Yet, as long as the decisions are ethically based, "doing the right thing" should be easier. The following are a number of useful suggestions for making good, ethically based decisions adapted from Zinn (1993):

1. Gather all of the information. Be sure to separate facts from opinions.

2. Explore codes of ethics relevant to your profession or to the particular dilemma. Just because adult, community, and continuing education does not have a code of ethics, don't stop there. Look at other professions such as medicine or law for ideas.

3. Examine your own values and beliefs. Remember, our decisions and actions are strongly influenced by our individual values and beliefs.

4. Try to do some critical reflecting about the situation; look at it from all sides.

5. Consult your peers and other individuals who may have more experience or professional training related to the situation. Talk it out with them. Consider different scenarios based on the possible decisions you make. Listen carefully to their arguments.

6. Trust your heart; sometimes following what your instinct tells you is the best way to go.

7. Look for a "win/win" solution. Avoid using fighting words and remember to honor all parties with respect and dignity.

8. Sleep on it. Give your mind a chance to work on the dilemma while your body is at rest. When you awake, check how you feel. Do you still feel the same way?

9. Make your best decision, knowing that it is probably not perfect. Living with the consequences of our decisions challenges us to act with integrity in every situation.

SUMMARY

This chapter looked at some of the legal and ethical considerations in adult, community, and continuing education. We started with an overview of affirmative action and equal employment opportunities and how these laws affect what we do in the hiring process. We then looked at the Americans with Disabilities Act and its implications for adult, community, and continuing education. Preparing contracts and putting things in writing was discussed next. Finally, we looked at the importance of ethics in adult, community, and continuing education and how to make ethically based decisions. We turn now to some ideas of how to be and remain an effective administrator in adult, community, and continuing education.

CHAPTER 9

Maintaining Effectiveness
As an Administrator

We trust you have enjoyed the journey thus far in better understanding how to be an effective administrator of adult, community, and continuing education. Indeed, the task may seem overwhelming, verging on the impossible. Yet, by approaching administration from a holistic perspective and seeing how the many parts of the puzzle lead to a greater whole, we are certain your efforts can be more than satisfying.

There are some additional aspects to consider in maintaining your effectiveness as an administrator and those around you, and that is what this final chapter is about. Renewal, growth, and professional development are all valuable elements in maintaining peak performance. This chapter discusses the importance of professional development as a means of ensuring administrative success. We talk about how to simultaneously renew and grow as an administrator and what you can do to help others in the organization work toward their potential. We discuss the characteristics of a learning organization and how you can use the precepts to improve your own organization. Attention shifts to preparing professional development plans as tools for growing, changing, and dealing with the daunting task of remaining current in the information age. The chapter ends with a brief annotated listing of resources we have found to be particularly helpful in ensuring administrative and organizational success in adult, community, and continuing education.

GROWING PERSONALLY AND PROFESSIONALLY

It probably isn't going to surprise you that we think the business of administration in adult, community, and continuing education is especially important. In fact, we are hard pressed to think of anything more important since the notion of shaping ideas, helping people be productive, and getting things done is fundamental to the success of any organization. In Chapter 1 and throughout the book, we discussed some of the essentials of administration in adult, community, and continuing education such as developing a philosophy and mission, setting goals and objectives, organizing and structuring the operation, leading, staffing, budgeting, marketing, and evaluating programs and developing staff. Now it is time to talk about how to keep ourselves and others fresh and updated so that our administrative efforts will yield the kind of rewards we are all looking for.

Very often in adult, community, and continuing education, success is measured by the number of programs offered, the numbers of students enrolled, graduation or completion rates, and the profits earned by the organization. Certainly, indicators such as these are important, but we all know that performance measures focused solely on the bottom line are dangerous and myopic if the efforts of faculty, staff, and volunteers are taken for granted or simply overlooked. In fact, the ultimate success of any organization is directly related to what people do, and finding ways of helping them grow and keeping current is fundamental if not morally right. A key question then is, What can I do to make sure my organization is marked by growth and development of everyone involved?

Looking at Yourself in the Mirror

In many respects, the answer to this question starts with yourself as a role model and leader within the organization. Are you a growing, changing person interested in exploring new ideas and challenges? Do you see problems as opportunities? Do you seek out various people within your organization for their ideas? Can you accept criticism and be able to avoid the destructiveness of taking it personally? Are you goal-oriented? Do you write a performance plan for yourself and monitor your progress frequently? Do you set time aside each day for your own benefit such as physical exercise, personal reading, and reflective thought? Do you regularly attend professional meetings, conferences or workshops? Do you have high expectations for yourself and know when you and those around you have succeeded? Are you an active lifelong learner? Answers to questions such as these tell a great deal about the kind of administrator you are and what you can expect of others. It is one thing to have high expectations for employees, but acting personally on an agenda of growth and development starts with yourself. Uris (1988) identifies four basics that describe the successful executive in any organization. As you read these attributes see if any apply to you:

1. **Mental fitness.** The capable executive has a broad-ranging, mature outlook in work scene. Values, standards, expectations of behavior and performance of others and of self are realistic—which doesn't interfere with setting high goals. An emotional tone is set well below hysteria and decidedly above passivity. 'The job' is considered the second most-important thing, the first, of course, the individual's own well-being and life goals.

2. **Physical fitness.** Good physical health is characteristic of those who are productive, although as has been demonstrated over and over, so-called handicapped people can be top performers. Generally, the health area is one we can help ourselves considerably. Advances in medical knowledge have increased our understanding of the role of diet, exercise, sleep, and so on. Also important is the raised level of awareness of physical fitness needs and possibilities. Regular checkups and proper medical guidance can extend life spans, and equally important, the persistence of youthfulness into what used to be called 'middle age.'

3. **Personal efficiency.** The ability to map out his or her areas of responsibility, and the work to satisfy it, is a conspicuous achievement of the good executive. 'Well organized' are among the most-sought-after words of praise.

4. **Self-image as booster.** One more major element helps foster effective self-organization. Successful executives develop a mind-picture, a favorable self-portrait that operates as a benign taskmaster (Uris, 1988, pp. 232–233).

The implications of this list are directly relevant to your personal effectiveness. Those who *wish* to achieve may do just that, but those who believe they will achieve considerably increase their chances. The choice is yours and we trust you will select the latter.

Creating the Learning Organization

During the past few years, there has been a growing body of literature stressing the importance of learning in organizations. As adult, community, and continuing educators, this emphasis may seem obvious or long overdue since so much of our business involves learning. In fact, many of the programs we sponsor are about personal and professional development, organizational change, and business efficacy. Yet, all too often, adult, community, and continuing education organizations turn out to be poor practitioners of the very concepts they represent! Many times our over-taxed workloads become excuses for not taking care of our own learning needs and those within the organization. Probably one of the best indicators of a healthy adult, community, and continuing education organization is the extent to which it systematically encourages and reinforces learning and growth within the organization.

In a dramatic departure from many of the management texts of the 1970s and 1980s in which *excellence* and *quality* were the words of salvation, Peter Senge (1990) published a book devoted to the art and practice of the learning organization. According to Senge, "It is no accident that most organizations learn poorly. The way they are designed and managed, the way people's jobs are defined, and, most importantly, the way we have all been taught to think and interact (not only in organizations but more broadly) create fundamental learning disabilities. These disabilities operate despite the best efforts of bright, committed people. Often, the harder they try to solve problems, the worse the results. What learning does occur takes place despite these learning disabilities—for they pervade all organizations to some degree" (p. 18). Senge identifies seven learning disabilities that inhabit most organizations, though they often go undetected. The seven disabilities are:

1. *I am my own position.* People focus only on their position within the organization and have little sense of responsibility for the results produced when all positions interact. Thus, all one can do is assume that someone else "screwed up" when things go poorly or someone else succeeded valiantly when things went well.

2. *The enemy is out there.* The "enemy is out there" syndrome is actually a by-product of "I am my own position," and the nonsystemic ways of looking at the world that it fosters. When we focus only on our position, we do not see how our own actions extend beyond the boundary of that position. When those actions have consequences that come back to hurt us, we misperceive these new problems as externally caused. Like the person being chased by his own shadow, we cannot seem to shake them.

3. *The illusion of taking charge.* Managers frequently proclaim the need for taking charge in facing difficult problems. What is typically meant by this is that we should face up to difficult issues, stop waiting for someone else to do something, and solve problems before they grow into crises. But proactiveness is really reactiveness in disguise. If we simply become more aggressive fighting the "enemy out there," we are reacting—regardless of what we call it.

4. *The fixation on events*. Conversations in organizations are dominated by concern with events: last month's sales, the new budget cuts, last quarter's earnings, who just got promoted or fired, the new product our competitors just announced, and so on. Focusing on events leads to "event" explanations. Such explanations may be true as far as they go, but they distract us from seeing the longer-term patterns of change that lie behind the events and from understanding the causes of those patterns.

5. *The parable of the boiled frog*. Maladaptation to gradually building threats to survival is so pervasive in systems of corporate failure that it has given rise to the parable of the "boiled frog." If you place a frog in a pot of boiling water, it will immediately try to scramble out. But if you place the frog in room temperature water, and don't scare him, he'll stay put. Now, if the pot sits on a heat source, and if you gradually turn up the temperature, something very interesting happens. As the temperature gradually increases, the frog will do nothing. In fact, he will show every sign of enjoying himself. As the temperature gradually increases, the frog will become groggier and groggier, until he is unable to climb out of the pot. Though there is nothing restraining him, the frog will sit there and boil. Why? Because the frog's internal apparatus for sensing threats to survival is geared to sudden changes in his environment, not to slow, gradual changes. Something similar happened to the American automobile industry in the 1960s, 1970s, and 1980s; through gradual competition, the Japanese auto industry increased its market share from less than 4 percent in 1962 to over 30 percent in 1989. Learning to see slow, gradual processes requires slowing down our frenetic pace and paying attention to the subtle as well as the dramatic.

6. *The delusion of learning from experience*. The most powerful learning comes from direct experience. Indeed, we learn eating, crawling, walking, and communicating through direct trial and error—through taking an action and seeing the consequences of that action; than taking a new and different action. But what happens when we can no longer observe the consequences of our actions? What happens if the primary consequences of our actions are in the distant future or in a distant part of the larger system within which we operate? We have a "learning horizon," a breadth of vision in time and space within which we assess our effectiveness. When our actions have consequences beyond our learning horizon, it becomes impossible to learn from direct experience.

7. *The myth of the management team.* The management team is a collection of savvy, experienced managers who represent the organization's different functions and areas of expertise. Together, they are supposed to sort out the complex cross-functional issues that are critical to the organization. All too often, teams in business tend to spend their time fighting for turf, avoiding anything that will make them look bad personally, and pretending that everyone is behind the team's collective strategy—maintaining the appearance of a cohesive team. Schools train us to never admit that we do not know the answer, and most corporations reinforce that lesson by rewarding the people who excel in advocating their views, not inquiring into complex problems. The consequence is skilled incompetence—teams full of people who are incredibly proficient at keeping themselves from learning.

These learning disciplines, according to Senge (1990), have been with us for a long time. They are historic fragments of societies and the institutions into which societies are organized. The same learning disabilities persist today and must be overcome. Senge believes they can be overcome using the five disciplines that constitute a learning organization. What are these five disciplines and how do they work in a learning organization? We take up this question next.

The Five Disciplines of a Learning Organization

For many years, efforts to build learning organizations were limited until the skills, knowledge areas, and paths for organizational development became known. What fundamentally distinguishes learning organizations from traditional authoritarian organizations that emphasize control is the mastery of certain basic disciplines. These disciplines form the core for understanding the challenges and opportunities facing organizations and consist of systems thinking, personal mastery, mental models, building shared vision, and team learning. To better appreciate what each of these disciplines mean, Senge (1990) asks us to consider the following:

1. **Systems Thinking.** Systems thinking is a conceptual framework, a body of knowledge and tools that has been developed over the past fifty years, to make the full patterns clearer, and to help us see how to change them effectively. Though the tools are new, the underlying worldview is extremely intuitive and quickly learned.

2. **Personal Mastery.** Personal mastery is the discipline of continually clarifying and deepening our personal vision, of focusing our energies,

of developing patience, and of seeing reality objectively. As such, it is an essential cornerstone of the learning organization—the learning organization's spiritual foundation. Surprisingly, few organizations encourage the growth of their people which results in vast untapped resources. The discipline of personal mastery starts with clarifying the things that really matter to us, of living our lives in the service of our highest aspirations.

3. **Mental Models.** Mental models are deeply ingrained assumptions, generalizations, or even pictures or images that influence how we understand the world and how we take action. Very often, we are not consciously aware of our mental models or the effects they have on our behavior. The discipline of working with mental models starts with turning the mirror inward; learning to unearth our internal pictures of the world, to bring them to the surface and hold them rigorously to scrutiny.

4. **Building Shared Vision.** The practice of shared vision involves the skills of unearthing shared pictures of the future that foster genuine commitment and enrollment rather than compliance. In mastering this discipline, leaders learn the counterproductiveness of trying to dictate a vision, no matter how heartfelt.

5. **Team Learning.** The discipline of team learning starts with dialogue, the capacity of members of a team to suspend assumptions and enter into a genuine thinking together. The discipline of dialogue involves learning how to recognize the patterns of interaction in teams that undermine learning. The patterns of defensiveness are often deeply entrained in how a team operates. If unrecognized, they undermine learning. If recognized and surfaced creatively, they can actually accelerate learning. Team learning is vital because teams, not individuals, are the fundamental learning unit in modern organizations. This is where 'the rubber meets the road'; unless teams can learn, the organization cannot learn.

The notion of disciplines is analogous to technologies in engineering innovations such as computers, airplanes, or automobiles. Senge uses *disciplines* to mean "a body of theory and technique that must be studied and mastered to be put into practice" (1990, p. 10). Chief among these disciplines is systems theory—the fifth discipline—that helps fuse the other disciplines together. By linking each of the other disciplines, systems theory helps ensure the whole can exceed the sum of its parts.

Senge (1990) captures the necessity of systems thinking in learning organizations this way:

> . . . vision without systems thinking ends up painting lovely pictures of the future with no deep understanding of the forces that must be mastered to move from here to there. This is one of the reasons why many firms that have jumped on the 'vision band-wagon' in recent years have found that lofty vision alone fails to turn around a firm's fortunes. Without systems thinking, the seed of vision falls on harsh soil. If nonsystematic thinking predominates, the first condition for nurturing vision in not met: a genuine belief that we can make our vision real in the future. We may say 'We can achieve our vision' (most American managers are conditioned to this belief), but our tacit view of current reality as a set of conditions created by somebody else betrays us.
>
> But systems thinking also needs the disciplines of building shared vision, mental models, team learning, and personal mastery to realize its potential. Building shared vision fosters a commitment to the long term. Mental models focus on the openness needed to unearth shortcomings in our present ways of seeing the world. Team learning develops the skills of groups of people to look for the larger picture that lies beyond individual perspectives. And personal mastery fosters the personal motivation to continually learn how our actions affect our world. Without personal mastery, people are so steeped in the reactive mindset ('someone/something else is creating my problems') that they are deeply threatened by the systems perspectives.
>
> Lastly, systems thinking makes understandable the subtlest aspect of the learning organization—the new way individuals perceive themselves and their world. At the heart of a learning organization is a shift of mind—from seeing ourselves as separate from the world to connected to the world, from seeing problems as caused by someone or something 'out there' to seeing how our own actions create the problems we experience. A learning organization is a place where people are continually discovering how they create their reality. And how they can change it. As Archimedes has said, 'Give me a lever long enough . . . and single-handed I can move the world' (pp. 12–13).

REALIZING THE LEARNING ORGANIZATION THROUGH PROFESSIONAL DEVELOPMENT PLANS

A fundamental characteristic of learning organizations is the extent to which professional development plans are used. These written plans are frequently negotiated by the administrator, supervisor, or volunteer coordinator to help explicate expectations for growth and development over a specified period of time, most often annually. Learning organizations use professional development plans or PDPs to help ensure that all employees understand the importance of self-improvement as a basis for organizational improvement. As Senge (1990) says, "To practice a discipline is to be a lifelong learner. You 'never arrive'; you spend your life mastering disciplines. You can never say, 'We are a learning organization,' any more than you can say, 'I am an enlightened person.' The more you learn, the more acutely aware you become of your ignorance. Thus, a corporation cannot be 'excellent' in the sense of having arrived at a permanent excellence; it is always in the state of practicing the disciplines of learning, of becoming better or worse" (p. 11). Choosing to be better is always the best alternative, especially in organizations that want to prosper and grow.

Preparing Professional Development Plans: Some Thoughts and Ideas

The preparation of professional development plans or PDPs starts with a commitment from senior leadership that they will be used in the organization. PDPs are somewhat analogous to annual performance plans used frequently in public and private institutions, but differ in two key areas: (1) they are grounded in a set of beliefs about human growth and potential, and (2) they focus on a limited set of annual performance activities related to the job, person, and organization. PDPs work better when there is a statement describing the criteria and procedures for employing them; this helps to facilitate communication and ensure clarity among supervisors and employees within the organization. (See Appendix B at the end of this chapter for an example of a professional development plan.)

SELECTED RESOURCES ON ADMINISTRATION IN ADULT, COMMUNITY, AND CONTINUING EDUCATION

The following constitutes only a small portion of the literature available on administration in adult, community, and continuing education. The literature is extremely varied and voluminous, owing to the many dimensions of successfully administering programs for adults. Works on administration and its many components including leading, planning, budgeting, supervising, managing, marketing, and evaluating are found in all sorts of books, journals, magazines, and nonprint sources. To provide some direction and order, we have limited the selections to books only that we feel are especially useful to administering successful programs for adults.

Brockett, R. G. (Ed.). (1988). *Ethical issues in adult education*. New York: Teachers College Press.

Brockett and his colleagues have written a very important book on ethical issues in adult education. Topics covered include ethical issues in program planning, marketing, continuing education administration, evaluating adult education programs, teaching of adults and so forth. Authors use case studies to illustrate the various dilemmas facing educators of adults. A very practical book that should help any administrator in adult, community, and continuing education deal with the vicissitudes of their practice.

Caffarella, R. S. (1994). *Planning programs for adult learners*. San Francisco: Jossey-Bass.

One of the strengths of this oversized paperback is its practical approach to program planning in adult education. Drawing on loads of relevant literature and her own experience as a professor and practitioner of adult education, Caffarella has assembled an excellent sourcebook for anyone looking to design and operate successful programs for adults. A highlight of the book is the "Interactive Model of Program Planning" that sets the stage for the program planning process that is described in detail in succeeding chapters.

Dean, G. J. (1994). *Designing instruction for adult learners*. Malabar, FL: Krieger.

Administrators should be involved in the process of assisting staff in the design of instruction. This book provides a practical and useful model for administrators and adult educators to use in designing and planning instructional materials and activities. Dean suggests that the instructional design process advocated in his book is adapted to meet the needs of adult educators. The book is filled with illustrations on how to use the model in practice. It is suggested that the instructional process detailed can be used in a wide variety of educational settings. This book is very readable and practical and administrators will find it a useful reference.

Edelson, P. J. (Ed.). (1992). *Rethinking leadership in adult and continuing education*. New Directions for Adult and Continuing Education (No. 56). San Francisco: Jossey-Bass.

Edelson and associates have crafted a useful book that challenges our thinking about leadership in adult, community, and continuing education. The authors suggest a new paradigm shift from a production-oriented organization to a learning-oriented organization. The eight chapters of the volume explore various aspects of leadership, emphasize the analysis of context from both organizational and individual perspectives, demonstrate how leaders can influence the development of their organizations by defining and expanding their roles, and provide some insights to leaders on how to prepare themselves to address the challenges of the future.

Galbraith, M. W. (Ed.). (1990). *Adult learning methods: A guide for effective instruction.* Malabar, FL: Krieger.

Galbraith and associates provide a practical how-to book on understanding and facilitating adult learning. Administrators who assist their instructors in becoming better adult educators will find this book a very useful reference. The first part of the book contains information on understanding adult learning and provides several self-administering inventories that help identify one's philosophical orientation and teaching style. Part two of the book contains detailed descriptions of 15 different methods and techniques for enhancing adult learning.

Knowles, M. S. (1980). *The modern practice of adult education: From pedagogy to andragogy* (Rev. ed.). New York: Cambridge.

This is a classic in adult education literature written by one of the "greats" of the field. Although somewhat dated, the book has many timeless qualities that make it a must for any administrator of adult, community, and continuing education. Knowles anchors much of the book in his work on andragogy, the art and science of teaching adults. Among the many useful chapters are those focusing on establishing an organizational climate and structure, assessing needs and interest in program planning, defining purposes and objectives, designing and operating comprehensive programs for adult, and evaluating comprehensive programs. This book is rich with many useful exhibits and illustrations.

Matkin, G. W. (1985). *Effective budgeting in continuing education.* San Francisco: Jossey-Bass.

Probably the most comprehensive book on the subject of budgeting in adult and continuing education. The subtitle, "A Comprehensive Guide to Improving Program Planning and Organizational Performance" describes the book well. There are many useful ideas on the essentials of budgeting including setting realistic guidelines and targets, achieving consensus in the budget process, and monitoring financial performance. The book features a number of actual illustrations that are applicable to any adult, community, and continuing education agency.

Mulcrone, P. (Ed.). (1993). *Current perspectives on administration of adult education programs.* New Directions for Adult and Continuing Education (No. 60). San Francisco: Jossey-Bass.

In this 10-chapter edited book, Mulcrone and associates discuss some "current perspectives regarding enhanced skills and competencies necessary for the adult and continuing education administrator (or manager or leader)." Some of the developments that are examined include how to utilize internal and external resources for program development, dealing with educational, social, and political issues, understanding the grant writing and implementation process, developing and managing budgets, utilizing unilateral and multilateral groups, developing effective staff development programs, using and managing technology, preparing and conducting evaluations, satisfying accountability needs with nontraditional methods, and putting administrative philosophies into practice. This is a very practical and readable book that provides some excellent insights and perspectives for the administrative role.

Senge, P. M. (1990). *The fifth discipline: The art and practice of the learning organization.* New York: Doubleday Currency.

This is an important book for any organization that wants to grow and prosper. It articulates a vision for seeing people as resources born with intrinsic motivation, self-esteem, dignity, curiosity to learn, and joy in learning. Senge takes the reader through a careful journey showing why classical management theories fail in today's world. He deaftly integrates actual case stories with analysis to help the reader better understand the necessity of creating learning organizations. Written for the general public, this book is a masterpiece that has relevance for any administrator looking to succeed in the 21st Century.

Simerly, R., & Associates. (1989). *Handbook of marketing for continuing education.* San Francisco: Jossey-Bass.

In every way a handbook, Simerly and associates have assembled the most comprehensive work on marketing in adult and continuing education. Its purpose is to provide practical advice to enhance marketing effectiveness of continuing education programs in organizations. The 33 chapters are grouped into eight parts including the components of effective marketing, positioning your organization in the market, effective direct-mail marketing, effective public relations, effective advertising, effective personal sales, making marketing work in your organization, and strategies for ongoing success in marketing. The book concludes with an extensive resource section that will be useful to anyone interested in improving their marketing in adult, community, and continuing education.

Sork, T. J. (Ed.). (1991). *Mistakes made and lessons learned: Overcoming obstacles to successful program planning.* New Directions for Adult and Continuing Education (No. 49). San Francisco: Jossey-Bass.

A gem of a little book, Sork examines common planning and programming mistakes that are made in the design and delivery of educational programs for adults and the lessons that can be learned from these mistakes. The book consists of eight chapters focusing on some aspects of program failure and what can be done to avoid such failures in the future. Emphasis is on ways of improving the programming efforts of practitioners in adult, community, and continuing education. This is a very readable and useful book that will be referenced frequently.

Strother, G. B., & Klus, J. P. (1982). *Administration of continuing education.* Belmont, CA: Wadsworth.

One of the first comprehensive textbooks on administration of adult and continuing education to appear in the 1980s, Strother and Klus filled a badly needed niche for students and practicing administrators alike. Using their experience in management, the authors prepared chapters on common elements in administration including assessing client needs, program planning, delivery methods and systems, program promotion and evaluation, developing faculty and administrative staff, budgeting and finance, and providing student services. This book continues to be a valuable resource for all administrators in adult, community, and continuing education.

Uris, A. (1988). *The executive deskbook* (3rd ed.). New York: Van Nostrand Reinhold Company.

If you are looking for a practical handbook designed to help deal with the many "mini-dramas" of the day, this book is for you. The book examines some of the latest management techniques and business concerns while providing practical information and helpful advice in planning, delegating, leading and motivating, improving personal effectiveness, decision making, and fair employment practices. Written in a clear and understandable manner, this book is a handy reference to keep on you desk. Highly recommended for its simple and eloquent style.

SUMMARY

This chapter focused on enhancing your effectiveness as an administrator of adult, community, and continuing education. We noted that renewal, growth, and professional development are valuable elements in maintaining peak performance. The notion of learning organizations as places that celebrate discovery, creativity, and self-improvement was discussed along with some ways of integrating the ideas in our own organizations. Considerable attention was given to the use of professional development plans as tools for building organizations where people continually expand their capabilities to understand complexity, clarify vision, and be responsible for their learning. A professional development plan used in continuing higher education is mentioned and an example is provided for illustrative purposes in Appendix B at the end of this chapter. Though specific to faculty, the format should adapt easily to your own situation. The chapter concludes with a brief annotated listing of some key books that we have found particularly useful in administering successful programs for adults. We leave you with these final thoughts: "Organizations learn only through individuals who learn. Individual learning does not guarantee organizational learning. But without it no organizational learning occurs" (Senge, 1990, p. 139).

APPENDIX B

Example of a Professional Development Plan

To give you some idea of what a professional development plan (PDP) looks like, consider the following extended example used in continuing higher education. The illustration is for faculty in a university setting where tenure and promotion decisions are based on teaching, research, and service activities. Notice that the plan emphasizes personal and professional improvement, articulates a philosophy for the PDP, states goals and performance outcomes of the evaluation, and specifies the criteria for determining levels of success. Although the illustration focuses on performance of faculty in higher education, the basic principles should be easily adapted to other contexts in adult, community, and continuing education as well as the preparation of your own personal PDP. Figures B.1, B.2, and B.3, found at the end of this appendix, provide forms for record keeping.

Suggested Criteria and Procedures for Developing
Professional Development Plans of Faculty

Preface

Regardless of our areas of responsibility as educators, the effort we expend will be reflected in the lives of people of this institution. It is hoped that the evaluation program will provide a way for each faculty member, and the Division of Continuing Education to improve. As we use it, let us set our goals high and strive to be the best.

Introduction for Faculty Evaluation:
A Tool for Improvement

The Premise

If enhancement of performance is to take place, it is necessary to believe that every person has the potential for further growth and development. Death is the only stopping point. This premise is basic in using evaluation as a means to generate improvement in performance. Both the person being evaluated and the one doing the evaluating have to believe this.

The Majority

It is well known that most faculty members are competent and effective in their jobs. Very few—often none—are sufficiently below par in fulfilling their responsibilities to be regarded as being unsatisfactory in meeting the requirements of their positions. This means that the evaluation process, for the most part, should be conducted to serve the needs of competent faculty. In this sense, evaluation becomes an important means to motivate further professional growth and development.

Some Beliefs

A few beliefs are basic: (a) every person, in cooperation with his or her immediate supervisor, should annually undertake three or more job-related, improvement-oriented, career commitments; (b) these commitments should directly relate to the individual's ongoing job description; (c) each person has some underdeveloped or undeveloped possibilities and potentials directly related to job performance and the "finish point," for an individual is never fully attained; and (d) career development must provide a great diversity of development activities and options.

Philosophy, Goals, and Outcomes
Related to Performance Criteria

A. *Philosophy— We Believe*:
  - that any organization to be effective must motivate self-improvement and be the result of a cooperative effort on the part of the person evaluated and the evaluator(s);
  - that to ensure that this process be a joint effort, the person being evaluated must have the right to dissent from the evaluator's judgments;
  - that the appraisal is to improve areas of individual effectiveness; and,
  - that performance guidelines or standards should be established to aid in the evaluation process.

B. *Goals of the Evaluation Process Are*:
  - to provide an evaluation program for all professional faculty members;
  - to make evaluation systematic, relevant to performance, job expectations, and a professional process;
  - to conduct formal evaluation conferences with records of conferences available to the person evaluated and the evaluator;
  - to clarify the performance expectations of individual faculty members by establishing primary job targets and provide opportunity for follow-up on "target" achievement outcomes;
  - to assess results of job performance both by means of self-evaluation and evaluation by the evaluator(s);
  - to identify various aspects of faculty performance (teaching, research, and service) for purposes of professional stimulation and growth—hence improved instructional programs for students (marginal performance identified and transformed into satisfactory accomplishment);
  - to annually evaluate the effectiveness of the evaluation program and revise it when necessary;
  - to establish appropriate ways for follow-up of actions needed for further improvement;
  - to establish both short and long-terms goals; and,
  - to involve students as well as faculty in the evaluation process.

C. *Outcomes of the Evaluation Process Should*:
- lead to an improved environment for teaching-learning of students and faculty;
- lead to a more effective utilization of the professional skills of all professional staff members; and,
- lead to future employment, placement, and promotion based on these professional evaluation guidelines.

Faculty Performance Areas

A. Preparation Competencies—The Faculty Member:

1. Shows mastery of the subject matter.

   Sample evidences: Calls attention to points of major importance; handles class discussions and questions easily; makes practical applications; is able to provide enrichment with extra information not found in class materials.

2. Continues to grow professionally.

   Sample evidences: Reads professional books and magazines; keeps up with current developments in his/her field; attends workshops and in-service training; recognizes the importance of self-evaluation and participated in professional evaluation of his/her teaching performance; and is constantly striving to improve his/her work.

B. Instructional Skills—The Faculty Member:

1. Creates effective learning situations.

   Sample evidences: Uses a variety of approaches in presenting material; is flexible in the classroom and utilizes immediate educational opportunities; shows originality in teaching; develops resourceful and independent study habits; is aware of the psycho-social and physical environments of the classroom.

2. Encourages student initiative, participation and creativity.

   Sample evidences: Students bring in outside materials; students do voluntary investigation and experimentation; students question and discuss, use committee work, plan exhibits, dramatizations, art work, and use a variety of source materials.

3. Establishes good rapport with the students.

   Sample evidences: Teacher and students are mutually respectful; teacher is consistently fair and impartial; is friendly and interested in students; is kind and courteous; creates a spirit of shared enthusiasm.

4. Nurtures critical thinking and inquiry.

    Sample evidences: Encourages and aids students who wish to investigate more deeply into class subjects; provides extra material for those who wish or need it; questions students in a stimulating way and treats their responses with a supportive attitude.

5. Provides for individual differences.

    Sample evidences: Familiarizes himself/herself with the backgrounds, personal characteristics, and problems of students; projects and problems planned around interests and experiences of students; expresses interest in and gives appropriate commendation to student effort even if small; gives time to help individual students.

6. Plans effectively and purposefully.

    Sample evidences: Clearly states both long-term and short-term objectives; uses well-organized short and long-term plans; plans are flexible enough to allow for inclusion of spontaneous learning situations; specific and current plans are written weekly; plans undergo constant revision in light of on-going evaluation of objectives and outcomes.

7. Uses varied means of evaluation.

    Sample evidences: Carefully observes students; uses learning contracts; helps students evaluate themselves; makes use of other evaluative devices.

C. Human Relationships—The Faculty Member:

1. Respects the worth and dignity of each student.

    Sample evidences: Respects the personal values represented in the classroom; celebrates diversity among students; treats students fairly.

2. Handles classroom appropriately.

    Sample evidences: Is aware of the emotional needs of students and assists them in solving their problems. Is *consistent in policy*, is firm but friendly, refrains from sarcasm.

D. Professional Responsibility—The Faculty Member:

1. Cooperates with colleagues.

Sample evidences: Assumes share of responsibility for the entire program; promotes and contributes to staff relationships; exchanges helpful ideas, methods, materials, and abilities with colleagues; recognizes and appreciates the contributions of fellow educators.

2. Exhibits pride in the continuing higher education profession.

Sample evidences: Adheres to the Code of Ethics of the Teaching Profession; participates in professional organizations; attends professional meetings and functions; is discreet in the use of professional information; recognizes that he/she automatically functions as a public relations agent for the profession.

3. Takes care of materials and equipment.

Sample evidences: Follows instructions in the use of equipment; and properly uses check-out and return procedures.

E. Personal Competencies—The Faculty Member:

1. Has a neat appearance.

Sample evidences: Dresses appropriately, is clean and well groomed.

2. Shows emotional stability and maturity.

Sample evidences: Is adaptable to change; adjusts constructively and maturely to frustrations and unpleasant situations; is able to cope with the unexpected; shows sound judgment; responds positively to constructive criticism.

3. Show enthusiasm.

Sample evidences: Obviously enjoys teaching, attempts to do the best.

4. Has a sense of humor.

Sample evidences: Can laugh at oneself, is honest, and can accept people as they are; shares humorous situations.

5. Shows a good command of communication skills.

Sample evidences: Shows adherence of ideas, both written and oral.

Sequence of Faculty Evaluation

Initial evaluation of faculty will be completed by the direct supervisor or by departmental peers.

1. During the academic semester the evaluation sequence will be as follows:

   A. Full evaluation for all nontenured faculty members.
   B. Partial evaluation for tenured faculty members.
   C. Faculty members who are less than satisfactory will receive a full appraisal each semester until achievement has either reacher a satisfactory level, or separation is recommended.
   D. Faculty may receive full evaluation each semester if they desire.
   E. All administrators in the Division shall have a full evaluation yearly.
   F. Students will evaluate faculty members at the conclusion of each course or more frequently if the faculty member desires.

2. Full evaluations consist of:

A. One preconference (to discuss teaching, research, and service expectations)	1 hour
Two classroom visitations plus follow-up conference	4 hours
One postconference (to discuss evaluation of the areas of teaching, research, and service and including the final written evaluation report. Student evaluations will also be reviewed during the postconference.)	1 hour
TOTAL	6 hours

3. A partial evaluation shall consist of:

A. One preconference (to discuss teaching, research, and service expectations)	1 hour
One classroom visitation plus follow-up conference	2 hours
One postconference (to discuss evaluation of the areas of teaching, research, and service and including the final written evaluation report. Student evaluations will also be reviewed during the postconference.)	1 hour
TOTAL	4 hours

NOTE: Times listed represent average time needed for visitations and conference, and can be more or less as needs would dictate. Visitations may be either planned or spontaneous as arranged between the parties involved.

Criteria for Evaluating Faculty Teaching

A. Teaching Criteria
   1. Preparational competencies
      a. Shows mastery of subject matter
      b. Continues to grow professionally
   2. Instructional skills
      a. Creates effective learning situations
      b. Encourages student participation and creativity
      c. Nurtures critical thinking
      d. Provides for student differences
      e. Plans effectively and purposefully
      f. Uses a varied means of material
   3. Human relations
      a. Respects worth and dignity of the students
      b. Handles classroom appropriately
   4. Professional responsibilities
      a. Cooperates with colleagues
      b. Exhibits pride in the education profession
      c. Properly cares for materials and equipment
   5. Personal competencies
      a. Neat appearance
      b. Shows emotional stability
      c. Shows enthusiasm
      d. Has a sense of humor
      e. Shows good command of communication skills

B. Each of the 18 teaching criteria will be rated and then averaged by faculty and/or students on a 0–5 scale, with a five (5) being equivalent to an A grade. An X may be used to indicate "no opportunity to observe".

The average teaching criteria score will be converted to a letter grade in the following fashion:

   4.0 - 5.0 = A
   3.0 - 3.9 = B
   2.0 - 2.9 = C

$$1.0 - 1.9 = D$$
$$0.0 - 0.9 = F$$

C. The quality of the teaching criteria will be evaluated by the following scale:
Grade of A = Outstanding
Grade of B = Very Good
Grade of C = Good
Grade of D = Satisfactory
Grade of F = Not Satisfactory

D. The minimum teaching standard is an annual average rating of "satisfactory".

Criteria of Evaluating Faculty Scholarly Output

A.

1.	100 points	Major commercial book
2.	80 points	Minor commercial book
3.	75 points	Editor of book
4.	50 points	Commercial curriculum kit
5.	40 points	National/Regional journal article
6.	30 points	Technical/project report
7.	30 points	Monograph
8.	30 points	Chapter in commercial book
9.	30 points	Research grant externally funded
10.	25 points	Audio/visual product
11.	25 points	Presentation of article/paper to national/regional conference
12.	25 points	Guest journal editor
13.	20 points	External research grant not funded
14.	15 points	State, institutional, journal article
15.	15 points	Presentation of article/paper to state conference
16.	15 points	Research grant locally funded
17.	15 points	Reprinted/translated journal article
18.	15 points	Written product resulting from official/ board member of state, regional, national professional committee, task force, or organization
19.	10 points	Local research grant not funded

20. 5 points   ERIC entry
21. 5 points   Published book/article review by faculty
                       member
22. 5 points   Faculty book reviewed by outside evaluator

B. Research output cannot be expected to exceed the time available to conduct research: $1/4 \times = 10$ hours/week or 40 hours/month.

C. Annual research evaluation points acquired on basis of $1/4 \times$ research assignment:

    30 points or more = Outstanding
    20–29 = Very good
    15–19 = Good
    10–14 = Satisfactory
    less than 10 = Not satisfactory

$1/5 \times$ research assignment:
    more than 20 = Outstanding
    15–20 = Very good
    10–14 = Good
    5–9 = Satisfactory
    less than 5 = Not satisfactory

Outstanding = 5 evaluation points
Very good = 4 evaluation points
Good = 3 evaluation points
Satisfactory = 2 evaluation points
Not satisfactory = 0 evaluation points

D. The minimum research standard is an annual average rating of "satisfactory".

Criteria for Evaluating Faculty Service Output

A. Service is defined as the provision of invited assistance, consultation, or involvement to someone, or a group outside the university regrading a professional issue, activity, or problem.

B. Service credit relates to the total clock time consumed by the service activity, according to the following criteria:

20 clock hours = 1/12 service credit, for no less than an academic year.

    30 clock hours = 2/12 service credit, for no less than an academic
        year.

    40 clock hours = 3/12 service credit, for no less than an academic
        year.

    50 clock hours = 4/12 service credit, for no less than an academic
        year.

C. Service activities might include:
  - Working with community boards—presentations
  - Working with professional associations—state and national
  - Presentations to groups—Fraternal, legislative, citizen
  - Serving on campus committees
  - Serving on state committees
  - Serving on national committees
  - Others

D. The quality of the service activity can be evaluated by the following
consumer and/or peer rating scale:

Outstanding = 5 points
Very good = 4 points
Good = 3 points
Satisfactory = 2 points
Not satisfactory = 0 points.

E. The minimum service standard is an annual average rating of "satisfactory".

As you can see, there is a great deal of information and detail in
the professional development plan illustrated above. We have always believed it is better to err on the side of too much information than not
enough, mainly because of the need to be as clear as possible. We also
recognize that sometimes it is better to give people room to experiment
with their PDPs using a variety of resources such as conferences, professional meetings, and personal readings to help push back the frontiers of
their ignorance. We hope you will see the value in using PDPs as tools for
maintaining professional competence of yourself and others while implementing the ideals of a learning organization.

Name of Faculty Member _____ Year _____

Name of Evaluator(s) _____ Date _____

Objective(s):   State objective(s) clearly; indicate desired outcome(s);
                  state how the results will be measured. Limit objectives
                  to no more than three per year.

1.

2.

3.

Action Plan: List tasks or activities to be carried out to achieve the
                 objective(s), including projected dates of achievement.

1.

2.

3.

Figure B.1 Professional development plan worksheet

** Comments of Person Evaluated	**Comments of Evaluator

Recommendations

** Please write on back of page or attach other written pages if more space is needed.

* Faculty Signature   Evaluator Signature

_____   _____

Date _____   Date _____

*   The evaluated person's signature does not necessarily indicate agreement
    with this evaluation report but indicates the report has been reviewed.

Figure B.2 Report of faculty performance

Faculty Performance Criteria	Satisfactory	Needs Improvement
A. Proportional Competencies		
1. Shows mastery of the subject matter	_____	_____
2. Motivates and encourages student initiative, participation, and creativity	_____	_____
B. Instructional Skills		
1. Creates effective learning situations	_____	_____
2. Nurtures critical thinking and inquiry	_____	_____
3. Uses varied means of appraisal	_____	_____
4. Provides for individual differences	_____	_____
5. Uses varied means of appraisal	_____	_____
6. Plans effectively		
C. Human Relationships		
1. Respects the worth and dignity of each student	_____	_____
2. Handles routine classroom problems appropriately	_____	_____
3. Respects worth and interest of students	_____	_____
D. Professional Growth and Responsibility		
1. Cooperates with colleagues	_____	_____
2. Exhibits pride in the teaching profession	_____	_____
3. Takes care of materials and equipment	_____	_____
4. Continues to grow professionally	_____	_____
E. Personal Competencies		
1. Has a neat appearance	_____	_____
2. Shows emotional stability and maturity	_____	_____
3. Shows enthusiasm	_____	_____
4. Has a sense of humor	_____	_____
5. Shows good command of English	_____	_____
F. Student Evaluations	_____	_____
G. Research Component	_____	_____
H. Service Component	_____	_____
I. Other	_____	_____

Signatures: _____   _____
                   Evaluator   *Employee Evaluated

Dates: _____   _____

*Signature implies only that the evaluated party has reviewed this report.

Figure B.3 Supplemental report evaluation criteria for faculty performance

REFERENCES

ADA Compliance Guide. (1990). Washington, DC: Thompson Publishing Group.

Andler, T. R. (1994). *Identifying and segmenting the low-literate adult population using geo-demographics: A model for community education use.* Unpublished doctoral dissertation, Florida Atlantic University, Boca Raton.

Andrew, F. E. (1989). How to find and select mailing lists that get results. In R. Simerly and Associates, *Handbook of marketing for continuing education* (pp. 179–188). San Francisco: Jossey-Bass.

Apps, J. W. (1985). *Improving practice in continuing education.* San Francisco: Jossey-Bass.

Apps, J. W. (1989). Providers of adult and continuing education: A framework. In S. Merriam & P. Cunningham (Eds.), *Handbook of adult and continuing education* (pp. 275–286). San Francisco: Jossey-Bass.

Apps, J. W. (1994). *Leadership for the emerging age: Transforming practice in adult and continuing education.* San Francisco: Jossey-Bass.

Barnard, C. (1938). *The functions of the executive.* Cambridge, MA: Harvard University Press.

Bausch, P. T. (1994). The impact of the Americans with Disabilities Act on university continuing education. *Journal of Continuing Higher Education, 42*(3), 10–15.

Beder, H. (1986). Basic concepts and principles of marketing. In H. Beder (Ed.), *Marketing continuing education* (pp. 3–17). New Directions for Continuing Education (No. 31). San Francisco: Jossey-Bass.

Bills, T. A., & Hall, P. J. (1994). Antidiscrimination laws and student affairs. In M. Coomes & D. Gehring (Eds.), *Student services in a changing federal climate* (pp. 47–66). New Directions for Student Services. (No. 68). San Francisco: Jossey-Bass.

Bolman, L. G., & Deal, T. E. (1984). *Modern approaches to understanding and managing organizations.* San Francisco: Jossey-Bass.

Boone, E. J. (1992). *Developing programs in adult education.* Prospect Heights, IL: Waveland Press.

Bounds, G. M., Dobbins, G. H., & Fowler, O. S. (1995). *Management: A total quality perspective.* Cincinnati, OH: South-Western College Publishing.

Boyett, J. H., & Conn, H. P. (1991). *Workplace 2000: The revolution reshaping American business.* New York: Dutton.

Boyle, P. G., & Jahns, I. R. (1970). Program development and evaluation. In R. M. Smith, G. F. Aker, & J. R. Kidd (Eds.), *Handbook of adult education* (pp. 59–74). New York: MacMillan.

Brinkerhoff, R. O., Brethower, D. M., Hluchyj, T., & Nowakowski, J. R. (Eds.). (1983). *Program evaluation: A practitioner's guide for trainers and educators of adults.* Boston: Kluwer-Nijhoff.

Brockett, R. G. (Ed.). (1988a). *Ethical issues in adult education.* New York: Teachers College Press.

Brockett, R. G. (1988a). Ethics and the adult educator. In R. G. Brockett (Ed.), *Ethical issues in adult education* (pp. 1–16). New York: Teachers College Press.

Brockett, R. G. (1990). Adult education: Are we doing it ethically? *MPAEA Journal of Adult Education, 19*(1), 5–12.

Brockett, R. G. (Ed.). (1991a). *Professional development for educators of adults.* New Directions for Adult and Continuing Education (No. 51). San Francisco: Jossey-Bass.

Brockett, R. G. (1991b). Strategies and resources for improving the instructional process. In M. W. Galbraith (Ed.), *Facilitating adult learning* (pp. 193–212). Malabar, FL: Krieger.

Brookfield, S. D. (1986). *Understanding and facilitating adult learning.* San Francisco: Jossey-Bass.

Brown, S. (1995, April 13). The debate at UW and across the nation on . . . affirmative action. *Branding Iron, 97*(101), 3 & 11.

Bryan, V. C. (1993). *Marketing programs and services.* Unpublished manuscript, Florida Atlantic University, Florida ACENET, Boca Raton.

Burnham, B. R. (1995). *Evaluating human resources, programs, and organizations.* Malabar, FL: Krieger.

Caffarella, R. S. (1994). *Planning programs for adult learners: A practical guide for educators, trainers, and staff developers.* San Francisco: Jossey-Bass.

Carlson, R. A. (1988). A code of ethics for adult education? In R. G. Brockett (Ed.), *Ethical issues in adult education* (pp. 162-177). New York: Teachers College Press.

Cervero, R. M., & Wilson, A. L. (1994). *Planning responsibly for adult education.* San Francisco: Jossey-Bass.

Cetron, M., Gayle, M., & Soriano, B. (1985). *Schools of the future.* New York: McGraw-Hill.

Cetron, M., & Davis, O. (1991, September-October). Fifty trends shaping the world. *The Futurist,* 11–22.

Charuhas, M. S. (1993). Utilizing unilateral and multilateral groups to enhance program development. In P. Mulcrone (Ed.), *Current perspectives on administration of adult education programs* (pp. 45–56). New Directions for Adult and Continuing Education (No. 60). San Francisco: Jossey-Bass.

Connelly, R. J., & Light, K. M. (1991). An interdisciplinary code of ethics for adult education. *Adult Education Quarterly, 41,* 233–240.

Coomes, M. D. (1994). A history of federal involvement in the lives of students.

In M. D. Coomes & D. D. Gehring (Eds.), *Student services in a changing federal climate* (pp. 5–27). New Directions for Student Services (No. 69). San Francisco: Jossey-Bass.

Courtenay, B.C. (1990). An analysis of adult education administration literature, 1936–1989. *Adult Education Quarterly, 40,* 63–77.

Courtenay, B.C. (1993). Managing the differences in public, private organizations. *Adult Learning, 4* (4), 13–14, & 30.

Cranton, P. (1989). *Planning instruction for adult learners.* Toronto: Wall & Thompson.

Cronbach, L. J. (1963). Course improvement through evaluation. *Teacher's College Record, 64,* 672–683.

Cronbach, L. J. (1982). *Designing evaluations of educational and social programs.* San Francisco: Jossey-Bass.

Cubberly, E. P. (1916). *Public school administration: A statement of the fundamental principles underlying the organization and administration of public education.* Boston: Houghton-Mifflin.

Cunningham, P. M. (1992). Adult and continuing education does not need a code of ethics. In M. W. Galbraith & B. R. Sisco (Eds.), *Confronting controversies in challenging times: A call for action* (pp. 107–113). New Directions for Adult and Continuing Education (No. 54). San Francisco: Jossey-Bass.

Darkenwald, G. G., & Merriam, S. B. (1982). *Adult education: Foundations of practice.* New York: Harper & Row.

Dean, G. J. (1994). *Designing instruction for adult learners.* Malabar, FL: Krieger.

Eble, K. E. (1992). *The art of administration* (Rev. ed.). San Francisco: Jossey-Bass.

Edelson, P. J. (Ed.). (1992). *Rethinking leadership in adult and continuing education.* New Directions for Adult and Continuing Education (No. 56). San Francisco: Jossey-Bass.

Elliott, R. D. (1989). Increasing the success of direct-mail marketing. In R. Simerly and Associates, *Handbook of marketing for continuing education* (pp. 141–152). San Francisco: Jossey-Bass.

Ericksen, C. G. (1993). Developing and managing adult education budgets. In P. Mulcrone (Ed.), *Current perspectives on administration of adult education programs* (pp. 39–44). New Directions for Adult and Continuing Education (No. 60). San Francisco: Jossey-Bass.

Fayoul, H. (1949). *General and industrial management.* London: Pittman & Sons.

Foster, K. S. (1989a). How to develop an integrated marketing and advertising plan. In R. Simerly and Associates, *Handbook of marketing for continuing education* (pp. 49–62). San Francisco: Jossey-Bass.

Foster, K. S. (1989b). A sample marketing and advertising plan. In R. Simerly and Associates, *Handbook of marketing for continuing education* (pp. 63–88). San Francisco: Jossey-Bass.

Freeman, M. K., Shaeffer, J. M., & Whitson, D. L. (1993). Ethical practice contributes to professionalization in adult and continuing education: The debate continues. *Adult Learning, 2*(8), 9–10.

Galbraith, M. W. (Ed.). (1990a). *Education through community organizations.* New Directions for Adult and Continuing Education (No. 47). San Francisco: Jossey-Bass.

Galbraith, M. W. (1990b). Attributes and skills of an adult educator. In M. W. Galbraith (Ed.), *Adult learning methods* (pp. 3–22). Malabar, FL: Krieger.

Galbraith, M. W. (1992). Lifelong education and community. In M. W. Galbraith (Ed.), *Education in the rural American community* (pp. 3–19). Malabar, FL: Krieger.

Getzels, J. W., & Guba, E. G. (1957). Social behavior and the administrative process. *The School Review, 65,* 423–441.

Gilbreth, F. (1948). *Cheaper by the dozen.* New York: T. Y. Crowell Company.

Gilley, J. W. (1989). How to attract radio, television, newspaper, and magazine publicity. In R. Simerly and Associates, *Handbook of marketing for continuing education* (pp. 216–226). San Francisco: Jossey-Bass.

Gilley, J. W., & Eggland, S. A. (1992). *Marketing HRD within organizations.* San Francisco: Jossey-Bass.

Griffith, W. S. (1991). Do adult educators need a code of ethics? *Adult Learning, 2*(8), 4.

Groteleuschen, A.D. (1980). Program evaluation. In A. B. Knox and Associates, *Developing, administering, and evaluating adult education* (pp. 75–123). San Francisco: Jossey-Bass.

Guglielmino, L., Frock, T., & Burrichter, A. (1988). *The adult community education administrator position: A job analysis.* Boca Raton, FL: Florida Atlantic University, Adult Education Division.

Guglielmino, L. M., & Guglielmino, P. J. (1994). Practical experience with self-directed learning in business ands industry human resource development. In R. Hiemstra & R. G. Brockett (Eds.), *Overcoming resistance to self-direction in learning* (pp. 39–46). New Directions for Adult and Continuing Education (No. 64). San Francisco: Jossey-Bass.

Hall, J. C. (1980). Staffing. In A. B. Knox and Associates, *Developing, administering, and evaluating adult education* (pp. 181–215). San Francisco: Jossey-Bass.

Hellreigel, D., & Slocum, J. W. (1992). *Management* (6th ed.). New York: Addison-Wesley.

Hersey, P., & Blanchard, K. H. (1982). *Management of organizational behavior.* Englewood Cliffs, NJ: Prentice-Hall.

Heyward, S. M. (1993). Student's rights and responsibilities. In S. Kroeger & J. Schuck (Eds.), *Responding to disability issues in student affairs* (pp. 17–29). New Directions for Student Services (No. 64). San Francisco: Jossey-Bass.

Holmberg-Wright, K. (1982). The budget as a planning instrument. In T. Shipp (Ed.), *Creative financing and budgeting* (pp. 23–39). New Directions for Continuing Education (No. 16). San Francisco: Jossey-Bass.

Jarrow, J. (1993). Beyond ramps: New ways of viewing access. In S. Kroeger &

J. Schuck (Eds.), *Responding to disability issues in student affairs* (pp. 5–16). New Directions for Student Services (No. 64). San Francisco: Jossey-Bass.

Johnson, D. M. (Ed.). (1990). *A handbook for professional development in continuing higher education*. Washington, D.C.: National University Continuing Education Association.

Joint Committee on Standards for Educational Evaluation (1981). *Standards for evaluations of educational programs, projects, and materials*. New York: McGraw-Hill.

Jones, J. (1994). Critical thinking: Is it reflected in your leadership? *Checkpoint, 1* (3), 1–2.

Jones, R. K. (1982). The dilemma of educational objectives in higher and adult education: Do we need them? *Adult Education, 32,* 165–169.

Kanter, R. M., Stein, B. A., & Jick, T. D. (1992). *The challenge of organizational change: How companies experience it and leaders guide it*. New York: The Free Press.

Katz, D., & Kahn, R. L. (1978). The social psychology of *organizations*. New York: Wiley.

Kaufman, R. (1982). *Identifying and solving problems: A system approach* (3rd ed.). San Diego, CA: University Associates.

Kearney, D. (1992). *The new ADA: Compliance and costs*. Kingston, MA: R. S. Means Co.

Knowles, M. S. (1980). *The modern practice of adult education*. New York: Cambridge.

Knox, A. B. (1990). Leadership challenges to continuing higher education. In D. M. Johnson (Ed.), *A handbook for professional development in continuing higher education* (pp. 35–54). Washington, D.C.: National University Continuing Education Association.

Knox, A. B. (1991). Educational leadership and program administration. In J. Peters & P. Jarvis and Associates, *Adult education: Evolution and achievements in a developing field of study* (pp. 217–258). San Francisco: Jossey-Bass.

Knox, A. B. (1993). *Strengthening adult and continuing education*. San Francisco: Jossey-Bass.

Kotler, P. (1984). *Marketing for profit organizations*. Englewood Cliffs, NJ: Prentice-Hall.

Kotler, P. (1986). *Marketing for nonprofit organizations* (3rd. ed). Englewood Cliffs, NJ: Prentice-Hall.

Kotler, P., & Andreasen, A. R. (1987). *Strategic marketing for nonprofit organizations*. Englewood Cliffs, NJ: Prentice-Hall.

Kotter, J. P. (1990). *A force for change*. New York: The Free Press.

Kowalski, T. J. (1988). *The organization and planning of adult education*. Albany: State University of New York Press.

LERN (1992). *Industry standards for classes with potential commercial content*. Manhattan, KS: LERN.

Lewin, K. (1951). *Field theory in social science*. New York: Harper and Row.

Lewis, D., Lewis, L., & Ponterotto, J. (1990). Legal aspects of affirmative action.

In J. Ponterotto, D. Lewis, & R. Bullington (Eds.), *Affirmative action on campus* (pp. 27–44). New Directions for Student Services (No. 52). San Francisco: Jossey-Bass.

Linden, D. W. (1995, January). The mother of them all. *Forbes*, 75–76.

Mager, R. F. (1962). *Preparing instructional objectives*. San Francisco: Fearon.

Mager, R. F. (1975). *Preparing instructional objectives* (2nd ed.). Belmont, CA: Fearon.

Marsick, V. (Ed.). (1988). *Enhancing staff development in diverse settings*. New Directions for Continuing Education (No. 38). San Francisco: Jossey-Bass.

Matkin, G. W. (1985). *Effective budgeting in continuing education*. San Francisco: Jossey-Bass.

Mayo, E. (1945). *The social problems of an industrial civilization*. Boston: Harvard University Graduate School of Business.

McDonald, K. S., & Wood, G. S., Jr. (1993). Surveying adult education practitioners about ethical beliefs. *Adult Education Quarterly, 43,* 243–257.

McGregor, H. (1960). *The human side of enterprize*. New York: McGraw-Hill.

Merriam, S. B. (1988). Ethics in adult education research. In R. G. Brockett (Ed.), *Ethical issues in adult education* (pp. 146–161). New York: Teachers College Press.

Merriam, S. B., & Simpson, E. L. (1995). *A guide to research for educators and trainers of adults* (2nd ed.). Malabar, FL: Krieger.

Metcalf, H., & Urwick, L. (Eds.). (1942). *Dynamic administration: The collected papers of Mary Parker Follett*. New York: Harper and Row.

Mintzberg, H. (1973). *The nature of managerial work*. New York: Harper & Row.

Minzey, J. D., & LeTarte, C. E. (1994). *Reforming public schools through community education*. Dubuque, IA: Kendall-Hunt.

Moorhead, G., & Griffin, R. W. (1989). *Organizational behavior* (2nd ed.). Boston: Houghton-Mifflin.

Morris, L. L., Fitz-Gibbon, C. T., & Freeman, M. E. (1987). *How to communicate evaluation findings*. Newbury Park, CA: Sage.

Morrison, J. L. Renfro, W. L., & Boucher, W. I. (1984). *Future research and the strategic planning process: Implications for higher education*. Washington, D.C.: Association for the Study of Higher Education.

Mulcrone, P. (Ed.). (1993). *Current perspectives on administration of adult education programs*. New Directions for Adult and Continuing Education (No. 60). San Francisco: Jossey-Bass.

Nadler, L. (1985). *Designing training programs*. Reading, MA: Addison-Wesley.

Nevo, D. (1983). Evaluation: What is it? In R. O. Brinkerhoff, D. M. Brethower, T. Hluchyj, & J. Nowakowski (Eds.), *Program evaluation: A practitioner's guide for trainers and educators* (pp. xiv–xxii). Boston: Kluwer-Nijhoff.

The new world of work. (1994, October). In special report: *Rethinking work*, Business Week, pp. 76–87.

Nowlen, P. M. (1980). Program origins. In A. B. Knox & Associates, *Developing, administering, and evaluating adult education* (pp. 13–36). San Francisco: Jossey-Bass.

O'Neil, J. (1995). On schools as learning organizations: A conversation with Peter Senge. *Educational Leadership, 52,* 20-23.

Owens, R. G. (1991). *Organizational behavior in education* (4th ed.). Englewood Cliffs, NJ: Prentice-Hall.

Patterson, D. M. (1989). Developing an overall public relations plan and budget. In R. Simerly and Associates, *Handbook of marketing for continuing education* (pp. 201–215). San Francisco: Jossey-Bass.

Patton, M. Q. (1987). *Creative evaluation* (2nd ed.). Newbury Park, CA: Sage.

Patton, M. Q. (1990). *Qualitative evaluation and research methods* (2nd ed.). Newbury Park, CA: Sage.

Popham, W. J. (1969). Objectives and instruction. In R. E. Stake (Ed.), *Instructional objectives* (pp. 32–52). AERA Monograph Series on Curriculum Evaluation (Vol. 3). Chicago: Rand McNally.

Porter, C. (1982). *Community education: Its development and management.* London: Heinemann Educational Books.

Porter, D. (1993). Improving administrative efficiency through technology. In P. Mulcrone (Ed.), *Current perspectives on administration of adult education programs* (pp. 67–77). New Directions for Adult and Continuing Education (No. 60). San Francisco: Jossey-Bass.

Powers, B. (1992). *Instructor excellence.* San Francisco: Jossey-Bass.

Provus, M. M. (1971). *Discrepancy evaluation.* Berkeley, CA: McCutchan.

Rados, D. L. (1981). *Marketing for nonprofit organizations.* Boston: Auburn House.

Ray, M., & Rinzler, A. (Eds.). (1993). *The new paradigm in business: Emerging strategies for leadership and organizational change.* New York: J. P. Tarcher/ Perigee.

Riggs, J. (1989). Determining an effective marketing mix. In R. Simerly and Associates, *Handbook of marketing for continuing education* (pp. 125–137). San Francisco: Jossey-Bass.

Romiszowski, A. J. (1981). *Designing instructional systems.* New York: Nichols.

Rose, A.D. (1993). Is there an ethics of adult education? *Adult Learning, 5*(2), 5.

Schroeder, W. L. (1970). Adult education defined and described. In R. Smith, G. Aker, & J. Kidd (Eds.), *Handbook of adult education* (pp. 25–43). New York: Macmillan.

Senge, P. M. (1990). *The fifth discipline: The art and practice of the learning organization.* New York: Doubleday.

Sergiovanni, T. J. (1993). *Building community in schools.* San Francisco: Jossey-Bass.

Shipp, T. (1982). Overview of continuing education financing and budgeting. In T. Shipp (Ed.), *Creative financing and budgeting* (pp. 5–22). New Directions for Continuing Education (No. 16). San Francisco: Jossey-Bass.

Simerly, R. (1987). The strategic planning process: Seven essential steps. In

R. Simerly and Associates, *Strategic planning and leadership in continuing education* (pp. 12–30). San Francisco: Jossey-Bass.

Simerly, R. (1989a). The strategic role of marketing for organizational success. In R. Simerly and Associates, *Handbook of marketing for continuing education* (pp. 3–16). San Francisco: Jossey-Bass.

Simerly, R. (1989b). Writing effective brochure copy. In R. Simerly and Associates, *Handbook of marketing for continuing education* (pp. 166–178). San Francisco: Jossey-Bass.

Simerly, R. (1989c). Setting up a production schedule and checklist for direct-mail marketing. In R. Simerly and Associates, *Handbook of marketing for continuing education* (pp. 189–197). San Francisco: Jossey-Bass.

Simerly, R. (1990). *Planning and marketing conferences and workshops.* San Francisco: Jossey-Bass.

Simerly, R. and Associates. (1989). *Handbook of marketing for continuing education.* San Francisco: Jossey-Bass.

Singarella, T. A., & Sork, T. J. (1983). Questions of values and conduct: Ethical issues for adult education. *Adult Education Quarterly, 33*(4), 244–251.

Sisco, B. R. (1988). Dilemmas in continuing education administration. In R. G. Brockett (Ed.), *Ethical issues in adult education* (pp. 64–87). New York: Teachers College Press

Smith, D. H., & Offerman, M. J. (1989). The management of adult and continuing education. In S. Merriam & P. Cunningham (Eds.), *Handbook of adult and continuing education* (pp. 246–259). San Francisco: Jossey-Bass.

Sork, T. J. (Ed.). (1991). *Mistakes made and lessons learned: Overcoming obstacles to successful program planning.* New Directions for Adult and Continuing Education (No. 49). San Francisco: Jossey-Bass.

Sork, T. J., & Caffarella, R. S. (1989). Planning programs for adults. In S. B. Merriam & P. M. Cunningham (Eds.), *Handbook of adult and continuing education* (pp. 233–245). San Francisco: Jossey-Bass.

Sork, T. J., & Welock, B. A. (1992). Adult and continuing education needs a code of ethics. In M. W. Galbraith & B. R. Sisco (Eds.), *Confronting controversies in challenging times: A call for action* (pp. 115–122). New Directions for Adult and Continuing Education (No. 54). San Francisco: Jossey-Bass.

Steele, S. M. (1990). The evaluation of adult and continuing education. In S. B. Merriam & P. M. Cunningham (Eds.), *Handbook of Adult and Continuing Education* (pp. 260–272). San Francisco: Jossey-Bass.

Strother, G. B, & Klus, J. P. (1982). *Administration of continuing education.* Belmont, CA: Wadsworth.

Stufflebeam, D. L. (1969). Evaluation as enlightenment for decision-making. In W. H. Beatty (Ed.), *Improving educational assessment* (pp. 41–73). Washington, D.C.: Association for Supervision and Curriculum Development, National Education Association.

Stufflebeam, D. L. (1983). The CIPP model for program evaluation. In G. F. Madaus, M. Scriven, & D. L. Stufflebeam (Eds.), *Evaluation models: View-*

points on educational and human services evaluation (pp. 117–141). Boston: Kluwer-Nijhoff.

Stufflebeam, D. L., Foley, W. J., Gephart, W. J., Guba, E. G., Hammond, R. L., Merriman, H. O., & Provus, M. M. (1971). *Educational evaluation and decision-making*. Itasca, IL: Peacock.

Szczypkowski, R. (1980). Objectives and activities. In A. B. Knox & Associates, *Developing, administering, and evaluating adult education* (pp. 37–74). San Francisco: Jossey-Bass.

Taylor, F. (1911). *The principles of scientific management*. New York: Harper & Row.

Terdy, D. (1993). Developing effective staff development programs.
In P. Mulcrone (Ed.), *Current perspectives on administration of adult education programs* (pp. 57–66). New Directions for Adult and Continuing Education (No. 60). San Francisco: Jossey-Bass.

Tyler, R. W. (1949). *Basic principles of curriculum and instruction*. Chicago: University of Chicago Press.

Tyler, R. W., Gagne, R. M., & Scriven, M. (1967). *Perspectives of curriculum evaluation*. AERA Monograph Series on Evaluation (No. 1). Chicago: Rand McNally.

Uris, A. (1988). *The executive deskbook* (3rd ed.). New York: Van Nostrand Reinhold.

Vialpando, J. (1994). *Affirmative action plan, University of Wyoming*. Unpublished document, University of Wyoming, Laramie.

von Bertalanffy, L. (1950). The theory of open systems in physics and biology. *Science, 3*, 23–29.

Walker, K. (1993). Values, ethics, and ethical decision-making. *Adult Learning, 5*(2), 13–14, & 27.

Walshok, M. (1987). Developing a strategic marketing plan. In R. Simerly and Associates, *Strategic planning and leadership in continuing education* (pp. 149–167). San Francisco: Jossey-Bass.

Watkins, K. E., & Marsick, V. J. (1993). *Sculpting the learning organization*. San Francisco: Jossey-Bass.

Weber, M. (1947). *The theory of social and economic organization* (A. M. Henderson & T. Parsons, Trans.). New York: Free Press.

Winter, C. (1994). *Planning a successful conference*. Thousand Oaks, CA: Sage.

Witkin, B. R. (1984). *Assessing needs in educational and social programs*. San Francisco: Jossey-Bass.

Wood, G. S., & Santellanes, D. A. (1977). *Evaluating a community education program*. Midland, MI: Pendell Publishing Co.

Woodward, J. (1980). *Industrial organization: Theory and practice* (2nd. ed.). London: Oxford University Press.

Zinn, L. M. (1993). Do the right thing: Ethical decision-making in professional and business practice. *Adult Learning, 5*(2), 7–8, & 27.

INDEX